Seven Days to Freedom

Seven Days to Freedom

Joining up connections in Creation

JOHN DUDLEY DAVIES

DARTON · LONGMAN + TODD

'Man is a "borderer", the sole inhabitant of a tract of country where matter marches with spirit.'
David Jones

'Man cwrdd nue fan cau allan ydyw'r ffin.'
'The border can release you or confine.'
Grahame Davies

First published in Great Britain in 2021 by
Darton, Longman and Todd Ltd
1 Spencer Court
140–142 Wandsworth High Street
London SW18 4JJ

ISBN: 978-0-232-53485-6

A catalogue record for this book is available from the British Library.

Designed and produced by Judy Linard
Printed and bound by Short Run Press Ltd, Exeter

Contents

A Summary of this Book's Argument

God is free. God is not tied to any human system of power or domination or control.

To discover the meaning of God's freedom, we explore the ways in which the themes of God's creation are connected together in the Hebrew and Christian Scriptures. We follow the working of God's freedom in creation, in the developments of the Six Days, with their increasing diversity; and this comes to its climax in the Seventh Day, with its mandates for human freedom in the laws of Sabbath and Jubilee, with a wide-ranging agenda for political and ethical commitment. But, by the time of Jesus, some of these laws had become ways in which people were being excluded, disconnected. In his ministry, Jesus was re-connecting people to the freedom of God. As result, he himself was excluded, disconnected, crucified; in his resurrection he renewed our connection to God's creative purpose. And that is our mandate now. God's intention is that this freedom should infect the whole human creation.

But this book is being produced at a time when our connections are newly confused. With new intensity, we discover how we are disconnected from our environment. The current pandemic, like the Great Plagues of the fourteenth century, like the pandemic of 1918–19, is making us more aware of the danger which we are to each other; we are exiled from our work, from our churches, from our friendships, and from singing. But we are also reminded how strongly we belong to each other. Like the Hebrew people, we can find blessings in time of exile. The story of Creation, the laws of Sabbath, and the Gospel of Jesus all tell us that there is a second chance for the failure, a place of recognition for the excluded, and liberation for the enslaved. If we want our doctrine of Creation to be true to our Scriptures, we will ensure that it includes and celebrates this kind of witness. In a time of loss and exile, our Creator's eternal purpose remains in place.

Foreword

If you have never known what a *cornucopia* is, you are holding one now.

The term was originally used to describe the artistic device in painting and sculpture of a horn-shaped vessel which overflowed with an abundance of good things, a horn of plenty.

And that is precisely what this book is: no turgid analysis of comparative understandings of ancient documents, but a revelatory compendium of contemporary truths culled from a reading of the Bible rooted in the realities of our day.

It is the fruit of the intelligence, insight, wisdom and compassion which have been hallmarks of Bishop Davies' long life and ministry, but it is written with the enthusiasm and worldly awareness of someone half his age. And that is because he clearly retains a love and passion for the Word of God and for people.

All the books I read are littered with squiggles, signs and symbols which are part of my conversation with the text. I cannot remember when last I read a book where so often I wanted to highlight, tick, underline or apostrophise words, phrases and sentences.

I offer but a few:

- Samuel is called when righteous people sleep.
- Jesus' favourite subjects at school must have been botany and economics.
- There is nothing in physics that is as marvellous and as

complex as the physicist; and the physicist is not more marvellous and complex than an urchin scratching for something profitable on a rubbish-dump.

- God endorses not might but right.
- Our name (the name of the human race) is Adam-*and*-Eve.
- It makes no sense to call a sheep 'unsheepy', but perfectly good sense, alas, to call a human being 'inhuman'.

It should be obvious from these statements that John Davies is drawing on more than theology. Here is biblical scholarship, the fruit of scientific and philosophical research, personal experience and the perspectives of others. John's first employment as a fitter taught him about the interconnectedness of things, and this gift is embodied in his writing. Thus he cites the wisdom of the ages and the diversity of humanity: Julian of Norwich and Richard Dawkins, the Scottish artist Margaret MacDonald and the Welsh-English artist David Jones, the present archbishops of Canterbury and Polynesia, Winston Churchill and an unnamed African-American taxi driver.

For me, the first chapter in the Bible has always been a source of wonder since, as a teenager, I read Dietrich Bonhoeffer's short commentary on Genesis. But what John Davies has done is to put flesh on the bones, to discern what are the necessary concomitants of believing that God not only made but loves the world. Thus he is able to elucidate how the creative process as described in the great Hymn of Creation which begins the Bible is not an alternative geological account of earth's development. At one point of detail he says, 'this may be bad biology but good theology'. It is indeed very good theology which has particular pertinence to our understanding of ecology, economics and true humanity.

Towards the end of the book, John explores the meaning of the Sabbath, that great gift of God to humanity which is not the end of the creative process, but its reason and fulfilment. The Sabbath, he argues, is not for inertia, but for genuine, purposeful rest, and for human and earthly liberation without which we perish.

The only thing missing from this book is a prescription for enabling other nonagenarians to be so fecund. In the absence of such a panacea, the book itself is proof that age need not weary but can certainly inspire.

THE REVD DR JOHN L. BELL
Member of the Iona Community, broadcaster,
author and hymn-writer

INTRODUCTION
A Fitter's Angle

When I left school, I was called up to the RAF, and was trained as an Airframe Fitter. In that trade, one of the images we would keep in our mental toolkit would be the hydraulic layout for a typical aircraft. A hydraulics diagram depicts the aircraft's plumbing system; it shows all the controls and functions, such as the undercarriage retraction gear, that are operated hydraulically. It identifies lots of pipes, all colour-coded, all connected together by delicate unions which are usually in almost inaccessible places, and always vulnerable to damage. They are essential for conveying energy from control to operating unit; and they belong together, as a network of connections. It was the Fitter's job to work with the diagrams and to ensure that the connections are properly in place. That was what we were trained for.

From this sort of education, I moved to university. Teachers there taught us about Subjects – units of information, such as Shakespeare's Tragedies, the Synoptic Gospels, the Metaphysical Poets, the Book of Job, and so on. A big difference, to me, between these subjects and what I had learned in the RAF was that the hydraulic system was essentially about Connections. At university, a Subject could be dealt with in isolation, and it was a matter for the teacher to choose how or whether one element of subject-matter could relate to other subject-matter.

The Bible is much more like a hydraulic system, or an electrical layout, than it is to any list of subjects. Even its division into Testaments and Books can be misleading. The Bible is a network of connections, of pipework in which energy is transferred from place to place, from community to community, mainly by means of songs and stories. And this is not true only of the past; its messages connect across different situations and communities in the present moment. So a main intention of this book is to discover Connections, Connections between different elements of the Scriptures, Connections with my own mixed experience of sensitivity and of missing the point.

Most scholars recognise that in the Bible as Christians inherit it there are two distinct accounts of the divine Creation. One, the first to be written, we might call the Adam-and-Eve sequence, between Genesis 2:4 and the end of Genesis 3, and picked up in detailed exposition by St Paul. A huge literature has developed in the interpretation of this account, and I have contributed to this myself. But it is the second account to which the present study refers. We might call this the Sabbath sequence. It comes in four stages: the Six Days of Creation, the Sabbath Day of Rest, the application of Sabbath in the Year of Jubilee in the Mosaic Law, and the reclaiming of Sabbath by Jesus. Each of these stages, separately, has been, over many centuries, an inspiring source of wisdom. There are studies in, for instance, the science-and-faith investigation, or on climate-change, or on the virtues of the Sabbath Rest, or on the healing ministry of Jesus; in this short study, I can refer to these only in passing. But, running through the whole sequence, there is a potent series of connections, and I suggest that the total significance of the integrated series is more fruitful than the sum of the separate elements. Throughout, we find a gospel of liberating grace and mandates of hope for the slaves, the failures, the excluded, and the building-blocks for a community of freedom. I have not found elsewhere any exposition of this integrated sequence, and so I offer this very slight attempt, in the hope that others will take this exploration much further. I make no claim to be able to pilot the aircraft or to navigate; but perhaps, as a Fitter, I can check whether the connections are in place and are serviceable.

Those connections provide a theme running through this book. I was minded, at one stage, to provide an illustration of the hydraulic system of a big aircraft. But I realised that this, though interesting, would not connect with the experience of many readers. However, nearly all of us live in households which depend on the effective working of the connections of electrical wiring systems; in principle, these are not so very different from hydraulic systems.

So I suggest that you take a moment to reflect on the electric system of your home, and on its dependence on connections, connections, connections – some hidden and permanent, some temporary and easy to disconnect. Without them, you would not be able to get the power to work for you, in kettle or TV; and, of course, if done wrong they can shock, damage, and ignite.

The job of a Fitter is not just about getting everything right according to the design on paper. Often it involves adapting, getting round things that don't quite fit, coping with uncertainty, correcting mistakes. Once, I was ordered to cut a hole about 6 inches square in the metal skin of a stressed area of a brand-new heavy bomber, and to make and fit an inspection panel. Ordinarily, for this sort of work they would have sent the aircraft back to the manufacturer, but there was not time for that. Making and fitting the panel was not a problem – if I got it wrong it was possible to make another. But cutting the hole accurately was quite another matter – if I got it wrong the whole aircraft would be disabled and out of service. And then I found that I had to do the same job on six other aircraft. That was anxiety. It was something like the anxiety of a surgeon. You devise a solution to a problem; and you ask, will it work? It could be seen as a parable of our problem with COVID-19, which even the former Governor of the Bank of England has described as 'radical uncertainty'.

So, to get into the main themes of this book, I suggest that you start by meditating on the connections that you depend on – those provided by the plumber, the electrician, the TV system, the Wi-Fi, and so much more. They are all parables of God's working with us.

JOHN DUDLEY DAVIES
Gobowen: Festival of the Annunciation 2020

1.
A Missing Connection?

In the very first story in the Bible, there occurs something which looks like a big mistake. It is not a mistake in the text, but in the organisation of the text. Eight hundred years ago, an editor decided that the first chapter of Genesis should end with the Sixth Day of Creation, and that the Seventh Day should start a new chapter. That editor was not a Hebrew sage but an Archbishop of Canterbury, Stephen Langton, who, as well as organising Magna Carta, arranged the Bible into chapters. The Archbishop performed a massive job, and all readers of the Bible must be grateful for his service in helping us to find our way around the text. But his arrangement does present the occasional problem. Let us ignore his chapter-division at this point, and read straight on from the end of Chapter 1 of Genesis into Chapter 2. Clearly, there should be no break. We can see that, far from being a new start, the Seventh Day smoothly follows what has gone before. It is the proper conclusion of the previous six. As Dietrich Bonhoeffer says of the Seventh Day: 'All the days of the week have really only been created for its sake.'[1] But our customary way of reading Genesis *disconnects* the Seventh, the Sabbath, from the rest of the narrative.

Both Jews and Christians live with the effect of the Archbishop's arrangement. Many interpretations of this creation story are based on the assumption that it was concluded in six days. Chester Cathedral installed a fascinating window, picturing days one to six, in their subtlety and variety. But where does day seven fit in? Josef Haydn taught us so wisely, in his oratorio 'The Creation', that we should sing about Creation before we argue about it; but even he missed the point. With innovative subtlety, he explored chaos at the beginning, seeing it not as scary violence but giving it an almost modern character of unpredictability, a formlessness where nothing leads anywhere, no cadences, and no fulfilled directions.[2] He adumbrated the Big Bang with his announcement '... and... there... was... LIGHT' – the most dramatic moment in music. And he has given us splendid songs and choruses celebrating the achievements of the Six Days. But where is the Seventh? What might he have made of the Seventh Day, if he had realised where it fits into the total structure?

Where I grew up, we were served by the northern arm of the Great Western Railway, running direct from London Paddington, via Birmingham and Chester, to Birkenhead Woodside terminus. I often travelled on this line; Woodside was only a fourpenny bus ride from home. Now Birkenhead Woodside railway station has been destroyed; there is no service from Paddington; the line from Birmingham terminates at Chester. The destination of the journey has been amputated; there is no mainline station for the 300,000 citizens of Birkenhead. No terminus. This is a parable of the structure of the first chapter of Genesis. When the Seventh Day is amputated, the Creation story similarly has no terminus, no destination.

At first sight, it may seem that the 'days' of Creation are a simple catalogue of different elements in our universe. But there is a more dynamic character to these 'days'; the process of each 'day' provides a mechanism for what is to follow. Each 'day' unlocks the potential for what is to come. So we can describe hydrogen as a light colourless gas, but it has the potential, given sufficient time, say thirteen and a half billion years, to become Chancellor of the Exchequer – or, equally, to become the manager of Auschwitz, or, again, to become the One born in a manger whom we know as Son of Mary and Son of God. The Six Days unlock the potential for the intentional ethical expansion represented by the Seventh. The purpose of this short essay is to explore some of the details of this structure, and to recognise some of the ways in which the Sabbath potential is released.

This is not a mere technicality of the layout of the text. When we see the relationship between the Seventh Day and the days before it, we can better recognise the relationship between the biblical vision of Creation and the debate that comes from scientific investigation. And, still more significant, when we see the place of the Seventh Day we can see that our doctrine of Creation carries a huge cargo of implications for our moral and political obedience. When we *re-connect* the Seventh Day to the six, we do not only connect to the basic idea of the Sabbath rest; we connect to a whole programme of social liberation which the Sabbath law carries with it. We can see the way to becoming a Sabbath-society. And we can connect with Jesus, the re-creator and fulfiller of the Creator's purpose. Such re-*connection* is the intention of this essay.

2.

Connecting at the Beginning

Although it knows nothing about the Second Law of Thermodynamics, the first chapter of Genesis does fit fairly neatly into the patterns disclosed by modern science. It follows a sequence, starting with a singular moment, followed by a fundamental division, then the development into increasing diversity and complexity; then life, with its built-in mandate to survive and reproduce; then the emergence of the human from its ancestry in mammal life, coming into being just before knocking-off time on the Friday. Science can recognise all this and, broadly, approve.

But there are discrepancies. What about Tuesday and Wednesday? Is this another mistake? We don't need a Darwin or an Einstein to tell us that you can't get vegetable life before there is sunlight – at least not until you can get down to the very lowest places in the ocean. At this point, if Genesis is intended to be biology, it is bad biology; but it is good theology; it shows that the text is not primarily about potatoes but about God.[3] Let us explore this theological contention of the Hebrew world-view.

The Hebrew writers treasured their history, the tradition that they were a free people, delivered from slavery in the process of Exodus. As a nation, they had been created by a liberating God, and they had developed the conviction that such a God was the

God who had created the universe, with a similar momentum towards freedom. But then there occurred a major catastrophe; their narrative of freedom appeared to be a lost cause. They had been wrenched from their home, transported far from their place of security in Jerusalem; they were trapped in Babylon, exiled as menial workers to serve a powerful, slave-owning, imperialist nation of intellectual inventiveness and political tyranny. There they sat down and wept – and cursed their oppressors in full measure (Psalm 137). But, enslaved though they were, they retained a fundamental freedom. Encouraged by Jeremiah, they could think and observe and pray and sing – the kind of freedom which imprisoned followers of Jesus were to discover, while the jailers were trapped in their role of being the imprisoners (Acts 16, 25; Ephesians 4, 1, etc). They could even wish for the well-being of the community that had trapped them, and pray for the Creator's blessing upon it (Jeremiah 29:7). And this would be a blessing in the midst of a cursed environment. This is the kind of freedom which Viktor Frankl was able to recognise, in the deadly context of Auschwitz, as a freedom which could 'give a man opportunity to grow spiritually beyond him'.[4] One of our most valued academic leaders in the struggle against apartheid, Professor Monica Wilson of Cape Town, used to tell her students, 'It's not what happens to you that matters, but how you react to it.' This was remembered by one of her students who found himself incarcerated on Robben Island; and he reckoned that the Professor had actually been speaking about herself and her experiences.[5] In this sort of way, Hebrew exiles could make a choice about the way in which they reacted to their oppressors. They could see that there were things that they could gain from their situation. In particular, they picked up some of the culture and doctrines of their masters, notably their understanding of cosmology. Their Babylonian conquerors had developed a sophisticated cosmology of the visible universe. The Israelites in exile found this made good sense, and eventually claimed that pattern of development as they composed the text which became the first chapter of Genesis.

But, however attractive might be the cosmology of their conquerors, those conquerors lived by a theology which was very different from that of the Hebrews; it was a theology of an array of supernatural beings that were constantly at war with each other, where the material world was a by-product of the hostilities between capricious divinities. It told of gods who exploited humans to do their menial labour; it promoted the worship of the sun as a divine power, and claimed that the lights of the heavens could control events on earth. Such a theology was, and remains, highly congenial for an enslaving society operating a system of tyrannical control; it tells us that we are victims of unalterable fates, and there is no escape from the powers that dominate us. The sun is a necessary power, but it burns without compassion; those who worship it find divine sanction for merciless cruelty. According to such a mythology, we are the playthings of supernatural forces which can do what they like with us – this is the cynical theology which underlies *A Midsummer Night's Dream*. Such a theology reflects and justifies the oppressive structures of society.

At this point, Genesis is defiant. It takes Babylon's cosmology as its frame, but into the centre of that frame it places a totally different God. It insists that the sun, important though it is as a resource for energy, is no more divine than vegetables. The sun does not create light; only God creates light. Only the Creator, God's self, is to be worshipped. The sun does not name itself. It is a thing of mindless matter. God names it, gives it identity

24

and value. Just as a Treasury official takes a lump of copper, zinc and nickel, bangs it into shape, gives it authority, and calls it a pound coin, so God, on an eternally vaster scale, calls things of matter and identifies them with a value of spirit. In recognition of this, Genesis puts Tuesday and Wednesday in the wrong order. The sun is in the same bag as carrots and cod, a part of Creation. Certainly, the sun is vitally important to us, a wonderful gift to celebrate and delight in. It requires us to recognise that, however clever we may be, we depend on something outside ourselves, which regulates our time and our energies. Nevertheless, the sun is still is a thing; it is not a mind, not a decision-maker, not a lover, and certainly not a god. A little child can know something about the sun; the sun knows nothing about the child. Similarly with the moon; just by being where it is, it controls the movement of unimaginable tonnages of water; countless little creatures are aware of its influence; its tidal effects produce the wetlands and mudflats which enable millions of seabirds and waders to exist and flourish. And, of course, the 'monthly' has its inescapable significance for half the human race. But, concerning all these things, the moon itself remains coldly unaware.

So, the sun and the moon have their place in the pattern of Creation, the order which Babylonian science could observe and which modern science can recognise and develop. But the valuation of this Creation, that is something which requires a valid theology. The theology of Genesis speaks of a single God, with a single creative purpose, and it tells us that, according to the valuation made by this God, the Creation is 'good'. It is difficult to see how a collection of adversarial divinities could have a common mind, to enable it to identify anything as 'good'. It might be able to recognise it as good to serve as a playground or a battlefield. But, according to Genesis, God reckons that the Creation, with all its components, is good in itself. It has its God-given right to be what it is in itself, irrespective of what human beings, which are themselves just another item in the whole cosmos, may think of it. Ancient world-views may suppose that the earth is just a battle-ground on which entrenched enemies, human and divine, work out their hostilities. Modern world-view may assume that the earth is just an endless resource for economic exploitation or, at best, human pleasure and enjoyment. The biblical world-view insists that the universe is the creation of a good Creator, who makes friendship and covenant with it for its own value, irrespective of human opinions; 'The earth is the Lord's' (Psalms 24, 50, 78, etc; Genesis 9). This is echoed in songs such as the Benedicite, St. Francis's Canticle of the Sun, songs from the Celtic inheritance, from Iona and from Bernadette Farrell. As John Bell of the Iona Community puts it succinctly, 'The earth is an older friend of God than humanity.'[6]

The sun and moon have purpose; they identify the passage of time. They provide the basis for calculation. Humans will devise other methods of measurement in due course. They will impose categories of calculation of length and weight and area and velocity and electric potential; in due course they will invent scales of value in finance and political leverage. But their ability to calculate originates in the given units of time. Creation happens in 'days' – in units of time, evening and morning, determined by the observations of sun and moon.

In the understanding of Genesis, a 'day' does not consist of 1440 minutes, but is a period of work, of activity, of Creation. In our western convention, the day begins with the morning, the sunrise. I wake, I get up, I go to school or to work, I come home, and the night is for me to recover from the day. For the people of Genesis, a 'day' is not morning and evening but evening and morning. The day starts with sunset, and then things happen.

God is nocturnal. Samuel is called when righteous people sleep (1 Samuel 3). The Nativity of the Son happens at night – the message to the shepherds, the visit of the shepherds to the manger, the communications to the righteous and silent Joseph, the star-guided journey of the Magi, and the flight to Egypt all happen in the dark. Most of us begin in the night. I don't know for certain, but I guess that it's most likely I was conceived at night – and that's most likely true for you. And afterwards, daylight happens. With something of a shock, I emerge into the daylight – or at least into the bathing of a light-bulb. In the Gospels, things continue to happen in the dark. It is at the Supper that the Son gives himself with his own hand.[7] The Death of the Redeemer happens when the sun is obscured. When the Son rises from the grave, at some hour before dawn, there are no witnesses, no infra-red cameras, to tell us exactly what happened.[8] The nocturnal God treated Pilate's guards as if they did not exist. Eighteen hours later, Christ the Burglar ignored all security precautions and found his way past locks and bars to meet his friends; he was with them, again at night.

It seems that this is part of God's habitual way of working with us. Nearly seventy years ago, in my own tiny corner of the universe, I was blessed with a somewhat similar grace. I had been, for several weeks, in a lonely darkness of depression and despair, occasioned by the loveless and cruel oppression that, for me and some of my friends, ruled both society and church; and then, hours after sunset, without any prayer or manipulation on my part, I suddenly was made aware that the Risen One was alongside me, knowing better than I the strength of the powers of darkness of the world; he assured me that he had mastered them, and he was alongside all people who were being treated as rubbish, as he had been treated. This was not evidence of any faith of mine. It was evidence of a much more significant faith, the faithfulness of Christ. He was being faithful to the same faith with which he had met people in his life on earth. This, for me, was his greeting and his peace. This was not a solution to any problems; it was something more valuable, a freedom, to be where I was, and not alone. This was not illumination; I respect and treasure the glory and mystery of the symbol of Light, but this was not about light, it was about the faithful companionship of the Son in the darkness. And from then on, that is really all I know and all I need to know.[9]

The Creator sets the boundaries of darkness and light and knows his way around them (Psalm 139:12). God forms both light and darkness (Isaiah 45:7), and they are both answerable to God. The darkness has its rights, its duties, and its space. In our little garden, I have a space which is remarkably good for runner beans. I know that they grow very well there. But, every year, I think that the seed is taking too long to germinate; the plant never seems to appear. But the seed is growing secretly (Mark 4:27). (Jesus may have been a carpenter by trade, but, to judge from his parables, his favourite subjects at school must have been botany and economics.) The darkness is doing its job, and I will only cause loss if I try to break the darkness to see what is happening.

For the most part, we fear darkness and reckon it as a hindrance to truth. But there are those who live in darkness and discover the God who himself lives there. Moses had to travel into the darkness to find God (Exodus 20:21). Just as the foolishness of God may be wiser than human wisdom (1 Corinthians 1:25), so the darkness of God may be brighter than human enlightenment. John Hull discovered this, in his slow and painful pilgrimage through diminishment of sight into total blindness. For him, the proverb 'seeing is believing' was simply untrue. Faith is about what is not seen (Hebrews 11:1–3). 'In a world where what is not seen is so often dominated, patronised, by what is seen, it is wonderful to read that in the order of Creation the unseen things have priority over those which are seen. Jesus' promise tells us that the sighted have no privilege over those who can't see (John 20:29).' John Hull's witness should warn us against the too easy assumption, to be found in some places in the biblical text, that such darkness and blindness are signs of the negation of God.[10]

The lights of the sky have their role. But they are not conscious, they are not divine. They cannot make decisions for us, and they cannot be blamed. This is confirmed in the Gospel narrative, in the first big story in Matthew (Matthew 2:1–12). The magi are sorcerers, who make a profitable living by being expert consultants for rulers; they are astrologers who assemble arcane calculations based on nocturnal observations of stars and planets. They have their in-group jargon and their specialist codes of interpreting evidence. They use their professional science to get political advantage for their sovereign employers. Isaiah 47 gives us orthodox Hebrew wisdom's verdict upon such manipulators of people's credulity. Such operators were part of the landscape in the days of the apostles – see Acts 8:9–24, and 13:6–12. Matthew's readers would know very well what sort of person was being described as a 'magos'. These salesmen of consultations and predictions make their living by persuading us that our characters and our futures are determined by the movements of mindless lumps of rock and gas millions of miles away. In our eyes, these men of the night are charlatans. But they find the road to truth; the Light of the world can use their dubious science to bring revelation into the heartland of holiness. They find their way to the Christ-child and hand over their wealth and the tools of their trade. But the truth is not where they expect. The truth is not in the star; it is in the baby. And that is what they acknowledge. Magic and astrology meet their master; rogues as they are, the magoi reach the Light of the world before any king or priest.[11] Their story echoes the defiant corrective with which Genesis re-positions the creation of the sun in relation to the rest of Creation. And within this theological discourse, science, qua science, does not provide assessment. In theological assessment, the lights of the sky deserve no higher status than do cabbages. That remains true, even in an age when we can feel reduced to insignificance by the discovery that our home planet is only a tiny item in our home galaxy, and that there are billions of other galaxies out there, and more that lie beyond the range of our perception, limited as it is by the speed of light. It does us no harm to be reminded that there is a lot in the universe which has its own reasons for existing, quite remote from our interests. At the other end of the spectrum of size, we are told that the size of virus which causes the COVID-19 pandemic, bringing so much disruption to our economy and our personal lives, is about eighty billionths of a metre – and that viruses are rather useful in preventing the universe from being completely taken over by bacteria – and we would not be where we are without bacteria. As Archbishop John Habgood has pointed out, chaos and disorder have been necessary in our evolutionary process. 'Biologically at least, danger is the spur to creativity.' 'The second verse of the Bible implicitly acknowledges the reality of chaos and boldly includes it within the creative activity of God.'[12] And, with great respect to the discoveries made in the disciplines of physics, it remains true that there is nothing in physics that is as marvellous and as complex as the physicist; and the physicist is not more marvellous and complex than an urchin scratching for something profitable on a rubbish-dump. And that is where you fit in, made in the image of God.

3.

Where We Fit In

Our Connections with the Rest of Creation

In the midst of their suffering and humiliation in exile, the Hebrew worshippers had good reason to believe that the human race was fundamentally divided into the powerful and the powerless, the exploiter and the exploited. They had also seen the evidences of the destructiveness of the natural order, of death by earthquake and flood, of cruelty and predation of animal against animal – the array of arguments which still for us, in our generation, constitute one of the greatest hindrances against believing in a good Creator. Isaiah was aware of this as a problem (Isaiah 11:7–9). His solution was that, in the Day of the Lord, when things that are wrong will be put right, the wolf and the lion will, in effect, cease to be wolves and lions, with the teeth and digestive systems which make them what they are. In that vision, their creation seems to have been a temporary mistake which at present mars the Creator's achievement. The correction of it will happen in partnership with the correction of injustice among humans – and it is an appropriate instinct which has inspired painters to depict representative animals to be alongside poor humans in greeting the birth of the Sun of Righteousness.

In spite of all the difficulties, those who crafted the first

31

chapter of Genesis insisted on affirming their belief in the unity and purpose of a single good Creator, a Creator who addresses humankind as a unity, who sees his image in our human face, who recognises no categories other than the category of gender, who does not allow for division by race or moral quality, who entrusts responsibility for the environment to the whole of human kind, who sees the Creation as 'good'. It is not yet 'perfect'. But that 'goodness' is the fundamental truth. In the daily prayer of the Iona Community, we 'affirm God's goodness at the heart of humanity, planted more deeply than all that is wrong'. On days when we are appalled by massacre in Manchester, shooting in New Zealand, or terrorism in churches in Sri Lanka, this affirmation can feel hard to make – but no harder than it would have been for our forebears in Babylon. This exiled downtrodden people found that they had a mandate to affirm to the human race its fundamental unity. That was a stance of defiance as absurd as the notion that eleven people could have a mandate to make disciples of all nations and incorporate them into the being of the one God (Matthew 28:18). A people who identified themselves as children of Exodus had a supreme spiritual alternative to the assumption that God is on the side of the powerful. They recognised that the power of the God of the enslaved Israelites extended over the dominating powers of Egypt. As our previous Chief Rabbi has claimed, 'nothing could have been more counterintuitive to the ancient world than the idea that the supreme power intervenes in defence of the powerless... This is the great paradigm-shifting moment. God endorses not might but right. For the first time, religion becomes not a justification, but a critique of power.'[13] God is not automatically the figurehead of empire and control. God is not propped up by Caesar. God is free, free to be God on the side of the losers. This freedom is God's character, which

God seeks to share with those who are made in God's image. The paradigm is further shifted in the Christian witness. Christ's message in the Beatitudes expresses congratulations (most clearly in Luke's version – Luke 6:20–23) to those who are missing out, who have nothing to show for themselves. We claim that God is not only on the side of the powerless but personally takes upon Godself the form of a slave and is treated as rubbish by the powers of law, religion and public opinion; God still remains God, but is a damaged God, retaining the marks of the nails eternally, and for that reason all the more worthy of our worship.

The message that God, in God's freedom, intervenes on the side of the powerless becomes the core belief of the Hebrew people. It sustained them when they were under the yoke of Babylon. It affects every detail of the Sabbath regulations which we will be considering later in this book. This interventionist God was, in Christian understanding, incarnate in the Son of Mary, free in his Godly dealings with the sick, the poor, and the excluded, including those authority-figures who claimed the Sabbath as a device for exclusion. The liberating God of Exodus is the God of the whole Scripture whom we worship.

We are correct, in these days, to be worried about the way in which the right of 'dominion' over the rest of nature has been taken as entitling humankind to exploit and destroy. If we accept that element of the tradition of the Hebrew scriptures, we should equally recognise their teaching that we should be humble before nature, that we should learn from nature's wisdom. Nature tells of God's glory (Psalm 19). The creatures of nature are our teachers (Job 12:7–8). Our singers and poets remind us of this. But in much of our practical application, in our western cultural inheritance, we have settled for a model of dominion, or authority, or lordship (which are all versions of the same basic idea) which is in accordance with the Babylonian convention of lordship, ruthless and despotic. Babylonian religion taught that people are made to be slaves of God and are therefore suitable for being treated as slaves on earth. Hebrew faith insisted that people, whether economically slaves or not, are in the image of God and can share in God's responsibility for the rest of Creation. The older Creation-story in Genesis tells of God's mandate to us humans that we are to be servants (the underlying meaning of to 'till') and guardians of the earth (Genesis 2:15). A spirituality which taught that people are mindless victims of cruel and arbitrary superhuman powers was declared to be false. That should apply whether those powers be a ruthless ideology, a circus of warring deities, or an apparently mindless financial system against which the poor can never win. At this point, Darwin is our valuable ally. He insists that there is one human race with one genetic identity, and our environment is a complex web of interdependent organisms. His teaching has been distorted and co-opted into support of ideologies of racial superiority and of economic competition. But his fundamental message accords with the Hebrew vision of the one human race, one humanity without reference to classification into friend or enemy, Hebrew or Babylonian, exploiter or exploited, believer or non-believer, Caucasian or Negroid, Methodist or pantheist; the only classification which Genesis here allows is that of gender; and even this is secondary to the affirmation that the image and likeness of God require the participation of female and male equally and together.

The notion of 'dominion' over the natural order is dangerous when it is picked up as a legitimisation for powerful landowners, for those for whom the hunting of wildlife is a privileged sport, and for those who have their hands on the levers which control mineral rights. But the first chapter of Genesis was not shaped for the encouragement of the domination-dealers. For the voiceless and disadvantaged to which it was addressed, the notion of 'dominion' was an assurance of their true place in the divine order. It tells them that they are not just mindless functionaries of nature, they are not slaves with no will of their own, who have to fit in with the decisions of the powerful. It encourages them to see themselves not as helpless victims of their circumstances but as human beings of rational responsibility, people who could be expected to care for their environment. It is part of a gospel to the poor. The Christian tradition makes this inescapably personal; it tells us that we take as a model of lordship the example of the foot-washing Lord, who was crucified and who eternally bears the evidence of this on his hands. That witness should protect us from the danger of misappropriating the mandate of 'dominion' and using it to justify our carelessness about the rest of God's creation.[14]

This Creation story is a theological miracle. It tells us that a true doctrine can be free to claim the imagery and terminology of the best cosmology that is available, while standing in critical defiance of the social, political and theological setting in which it finds itself. In all its majesty and splendour, the story of our creation, according to this section of Genesis, is rooted in a deep experience of suffering. At the very beginning of our Bible, it testifies to the creative adaptability of the human spirit created in the image of God.

4.

The Witness of the Sixth Day

Our Connections with our Ancestors

At the end of the Sixth Day, we have the creation of the human. For scientific humanism, this is the terminus, the climax. And this would also be true for Genesis, if we stopped at that point, in the way that the chapter-division suggests. But in the complete Genesis account, the creation of the human is indeed the end of a crescendo, but the climax is day seven. And that is theology; and it is a point at which science, again, has no jurisdiction. The arguments with which promoters of various stances discuss the credibility of the details of the Six Days are all very interesting; but, in the end of the day, they are beside the point. They are not what the text is fundamentally about. To grasp the total significance of the Six Days we have to wait for the Seventh, the day which is outside the range of the sciences.

However, it is still worthwhile to pause and consider what is going on in that vital stage of the Friday afternoon, the creation of the human. Although this is indeed just a continuation of the making of mammals, it is something truly new, a discontinuity as well as a continuity. There is a change of verb; whereas the previous things are 'made', the human is 'created'. A being has appeared which can be mandated to do more than survive and reproduce; this being can be addressed as a moral being, which can make choices and take responsibility. It may be impossible to assign a date to this novelty; but somewhere, at some time in the evolution of our species, a creature came into being who possessed not only the various physical features which we identify as human – the bipedal stance, the opposable thumb, the big and complex brain, and so on – but also some moral sense. *We* arrived. Our name is Adam-and-Eve.

There is no fossil evidence, no identifiable genetic mutation, to record our arrival, in this sense. But approximate dates can be given for the emergence of a similar arrival in our human history. Dr Jenifer Baker notes 'the evolutionary sudden emergence of self-aware, art-making human beings, as implied by the proliferation of cave paintings in south-west Europe from the period 30–40.000BP'.[15] Visible 'Culture' starts to emerge from 'Nature'. Dr Baker quotes the theological interpretation of this evolution by Dr Robert Jenson, 'Who were Adam and Eve? They were the first hominid group who by ritual action were embodied before God, made personally available to him... The painters were human, as we may know simply from the fact of their ritual. By the very act of giving visibility to wishes directed beyond themselves. They nevertheless in fact gave up control and worshipped.'[16]

So it would appear that the human capabilities of artistic expression, of awareness and worship of that which is beyond, and of moral responsibility, belong closely together. The emergence of these faculties has been made possible by an evolutionary process which produces evidences which can be identified and dated. But they belong to a being which is not limited to its biological processes. There are no genes which regulate our artistic capability or our moral identity. Genes for incurring guilt do not exist, any more than genes for propounding theories of evolution, or for composing the B minor Mass, or for managing high finance, or for organising Auschwitz. Perhaps, in future, that last sentence may be seen as an over-statement; but it will still remain true that we are more than can be attributed *only* to genetic inheritance. We need to be on the look-out for misplaced 'onlies'. As Hendrik Willem van Loon says, after extensive study of the operations of great artists, including Rembrandt, 'Genius in art is the perfection of technique, plus something else' – and Dr Baker's work is a fine example of detailed exploration of what that 'something else' can be.[17] Similarly, we will continue to insist that we humans are the product of our genetic inheritance, plus something else. We are creatures which can be given mandates and responsibilities; and we can say No. For the first time, a being has appeared which can contradict itself. It makes no sense to call a sheep unsheepy; but it makes perfectly good sense, alas, to call a human being inhuman. This is the message to us of the Sixth Day.

The physical equipment which science can measure is essential to this bundle of cultural awareness. Compared with most other creatures, we have little to show for ourselves. We have not gone in for talons or tails, wings, shells, horns or fangs. We shall look like undeveloped embryos until we die.[18] We are pretty good at grasping and running. We can eat almost anything, but so can hedgehogs, seagulls, and bears. We specialise in adaptability – we have managed to live in almost every possible habitat on earth. So we have been able to become the most widely-distributed predators on earth.

Our best specialist ability is not externally noticeable; it is our ability to think. We have inconveniently big brains, which give a rough ride to our females as they give birth to us.[19] These brains have been developed by countless generations of creatures engaged in the struggle for survival, in fulfilment of the mandate to be fruitful and multiply. Success in that struggle has gone to those whose male members have been good at two effective strategies, namely murder and adultery.[20] But now this genetic inheritance has unlocked a potential for a new creation; it has enabled our unique self-consciousness and human communication equipment, so we have a new and very powerful method of passing on our inheritance of information and behaviour. We become what we are not only by genetic inheritance but by the transmission of learning, for which the shorthand word is 'culture'. Our brains are now required to cope with an alternative mandate. In Genesis, God addresses us as beings who can follow a different programme, of responsibility and caring for our companions in the created environment. Survival and reproduction remain immensely powerful drives; but they are not the only animators of our decisions; we can stand aside and assess them. We can insist that righteousness remains righteousness even when it does not triumph, that forgiveness and mercy are worth cherishing even when they stand in the way of our own survival.

The instinct to murder is not far from the life-experience of every person. Augustine was one of the rare saints who was able to observe the behaviour of his own offspring. Noting the murderous attitudes sometimes displayed by the very young, he says that if babies are innocent, this is not because of any lack of will to do harm but for lack of muscular ability.[21] On the whole we, as individuals, do grow up. Can we imagine, perhaps, that our propensity for going to war is just an infantile stage in our corporate human development? Are we growing up? The evidence suggests that our development is still in the opposite direction.

The activities which God's law condemns as murder and adultery have been part of the struggle for survival for our ancestors; they have helped to build a successful species. But they are bad for the survival of community; 'I am the Lord your God who has set you free, therefore...' (Exodus 20:2; Deuteronomy 5:6). This primary statement leads into the Ten Commandments; they are mandates for a liberated community, given to enable that community to continue in freedom.

So can we base our social and political values on the factors which have brought us to where we are? Science does not speak with one voice. The biologists have every right to explore and describe the processes by which, in biological terms, we have become what we are. But as biologists 'they are no better placed than the rest of us for dealing with the problem presented by our sense of right and wrong, and we need not be surprised that in this matter they are not all of one mind'.[22] That sentence is quoted from a lecture given by my first teacher of theology in Cambridge sixty years ago, celebrating the centenary of Darwin's *The Origin of Species*. At that time, the Double Helix was no more than a glint in the eyes of Rosalind Franklin and Watson and Crick. Since then, the discovery of the DNA structure has, in the first place, been the most exciting event in biology in the twentieth century, and now has settled to become a routine feature of police work. Darwin's science has made huge contribution to our understanding of human origins and of genetically-inherited characteristics. But Burnaby's scepticism concerning the ability of that discipline to enable us to distinguish right from wrong is still valid. It does not offer a unanimous verdict. With twentieth-century optimism, Sir Julian Huxley saw ethics as a natural development of the evolutionary momentum. 'Anything which permits or promotes open development is right, anything which frustrates development is wrong.'[23] But his grandfather, T. H. Huxley, Darwin's colleague, was probably on surer ground when he claimed that, 'The ethical progress of society depends not on imitating the cosmic process, still less on running away from it, but on combating it. Virtue's influence is directed not so much to the survival of the fittest as to the fitting of as many as possible to survive.'[24] More recently, we get the same message from Richard Dawkins: 'Let us try to teach generosity and altruism, because we are born selfish. Let us understand what our own selfish genes are up to, because we may then at least have the chance to upset their designs, something that no other species has aspired to do. We alone on earth can rebel against the tyranny of our selfish replicators.'[25] We shall see a flowering of this vision in the mandates of the Seventh Day; but the creation of the responsible conscience is there already in the Sixth. And that can be dated back to considerably earlier than the twentieth century. We cannot claim that our cultural development has kept pace with the development which can be mapped out by science. Burnaby went on to ask:

'Who shall say whether in the work of man's hands there has been more of beauty than of ugliness, in the works of his mind more of truth and sincerity than of lying and deceit? Which is more typical of man's inventiveness – the great hospital, furnished by medical research with its innumerable devices for the treatment of disease and the relief of pain, or the intercontinental rocket, product of the frenzied urge to be foremost in destructive power? Which tells us more about human nature – the thousands of gallows upon which imperial Rome strung up rebels against her dominion, or the faith, hope, and charity which fastened a Jewish carpenter upon one of them?'

Perhaps in our law-making we have become more aware of our potential for destruction. We have succeeded in identifying murder as a sin. British law now reckons that causing death by dangerous driving is equivalent to manslaughter. But we have a long way to go before we outlaw corporate murder, for instance multiple deaths in warfare. I speak as a child of the inter-war years of last century. My father had signed up in a form of Army Cadets at the time of the war that the British call the Boer War. The training that they were given was 'in order to kill the enemy'. Our enemies then were people whom we now know as Afrikaners. Then for at least two years of World War I he was in the Army in France. Then it was my turn; I had four years in the Army Cadets, learning how to kill people. And then three years in the RAF, where my trade, a worthy and skilled trade, was in maintaining and repairing aircraft, designed and built to be more efficient at destroying and killing than those of the enemy. The twentieth century saw the most costly forms of world-wide war; but the nations of Europe had been bent on dominating or destroying each other for centuries before that. After 1945, national leaders realised that we needed some formal structures to tie the nations of Europe so strongly together by economic and cultural ties that they could no longer be drawn into programmes of destroying each other. That was a purpose in the formation of the European Union. And so, my children's turn hasn't come; and I feel passionately thankful that my children and grandchildren have not been required to learn how to kill people. But now, it would seem, we are losing confidence in such a venture, and the attractions of international murdering may start to flourish again.

As well as being a breach of the sixth commandment, war is the most destructive contravention of the mandate of the Sixth Day of Creation. God claims the right to arrange for the care of the world, which is God's. 'The earth is the Lord's and all that is in it' (Psalm 24:1). That is the headline message of the whole Hebrew scripture. God says, 'You – the whole human race – are in charge of the earth; you are to look after it and to be accountable for it'. But, in effect, we humans have preferred to adopt a Babylonian theology, a theology of many gods, and many authorities in continual conflict with each other; so we give our allegiance to our separate nations. The nations imitate each other in the search for separate wealth and separate status. That is our history, at least in the last five hundred years in Europe. Modern war does massive damage to the planet; war gives excuse for the destruction of the earth and for reckless use of consumables and fuels. This may sound like a pointless statement of the obvious; but all our reminiscences and replayings of the stories of the Wars of the twentieth century affirm one inescapable fact – the sheer colossal cost of war and of our methods of conducting wars. War is a conspiracy of de-creation. Even in a so-called 'peacetime', one military adventure can undo years of people's patient attempts to be careful of their carbon footprint. At this point, God speaks to us through the voices of the unborn. The theology of the Sixth Day tells us that there is one God; the mandate of the Sixth Day tells us that we are one humanity. By this we detect the measure of our unbelief.

War, armed conflict, is only the most expensive and most obvious way in which the mandate of the Sixth Day is disobeyed. Once in my life, in the early 1970s, my duties required me to visit the United States. For many of its citizens, this was at a time of disappointment and fear for the future. But I value the memory of one encounter, with a courteous and forthright black man, a taxi-driver. Concerning the landing on the moon, he started with some well-rehearsed words of dissociation from that whole venture – 'putting our nice white men on our nice white moon'. But then he observed: 'If you go to a place, and have to take everything with you that you need, even the air, that shows that you have no right to be there.' Since those days, that man's insight has in practice been followed; scientists have recognised that humans, with their need for fuel and maintenance, are an extravagant liability in space, and that it makes more sense to use machines that can cope with the violent extremes of temperature that are to be found there. The message of Genesis on the Sixth Day is that God provides all that we need, as a gift. We don't have to compete for it, grasp it, plunder it, score points off each other with it, wrest it from each other. What was the guiding motive of the moon-landing? International rivalry, on a hugely expensive scale. What we possess on earth we possess as gift, not as reward for our goodness or cleverness. Those who inherit the earth are 'the meek' – those who recognise that their possession and their responsibility come from the grace of their Creator. 'Once we lose our humility,' says Pope Francis, 'and become enthralled by the possibility of limitless mastery over everything, we inevitably end up harming society and the environment.'[26]

The mandate of the Sixth Day addresses humans as 'male and female' together. It states the Creator's intention for the human creation. How it works out – or doesn't work out – varies greatly between different cultural conditions. For instance, we cannot escape the obvious fact that warfare splits the 'together'. It is essentially a male enterprise. The Scriptures take it for granted that springtime is, normally and naturally, the season when 'kings go out to battle' (2 Samuel 11:1). They do what kings are expected to do. They make the land desolate. Then, when they are exhausted, we can hear a beautiful message of a Sabbath-state for the land – 'the land had rest for forty years' (Judges 5:31). It is not only military rivalries which display our carelessness for the well-being of the land. When a tall building is destroyed or reckoned to be redundant, does the land have any rest? Economic rivalry dictates that it will have to bear a still taller one.

There are, of course, female heroines in war, like Jael (who has to be identified as the wife attached to Heber the Kenite; Judges 4 and 5), and Judith, and Boudicca, and Elizabeth I, who caused their own share of bloodshed; but their battles have been in conflicts started by men. In wartime, as we have experienced it since the days of Florence Nightingale, a main role of women is to repair the damage which men do to men.

Men do what they do because they have so much spare time which is not claimed by the mandate to be fruitful and multiply. An African woman passed on to me the almost proverbial question in her community: 'What are men for, apart from giving occasional help in making babies and in moving heavy furniture?' It is strange that the system permits there to be so many of us males – no sheep-farmer would retain as many rams as ewes. So, as well as being in business to respond to destruction with destruction, we men have time to organise laws and traditions which function to protect the interests of men – and to write books about it.

In rural South Africa as we knew it, many children grew up in a female world. There was not much 'together'. The men would be away in the mines as contract labour, living in compounds or barracks with casual women companions; or else they would be in prison, convicted for technical offences against the pass laws – laws for which the unspoken justification was that they provided a reliable source of virtually slave labour on prison farms, of which I had about sixteen in my parish. So the sight of an adult male would be a rarity, except for the broken old men for whom the labour system had no further use. Women were providing the essential energies, of both body and mind, for life to go on and to Get Things Done. There were some 'liberal' white people who argued that there should be a qualified franchise for 'suitable' black people that black people should be allowed to vote if they could show that they had certain resources in wealth or education. Our answer was that a woman who had brought up six children in a tin shack and living, as we used to say, on the smell of an oil-rag, could have better understanding of practical economics than a graduate from the LSE.

Women like that are often the central figures in their community, and the core leaders. In local churches, they are the primary ally of the clergy – or, if the clergy are not wise enough, their main threat. They are the reason why, often, the Mothers' Union, rather than the official Church Council, is the most effective Christian agency in the community. Concerning international aid, there are occasional complaints that inter-governmental funding goes to the wrong people or to unsuitable projects. If so, it's because decisions are made by men in suits in large buildings, not by people on the ground. The Mothers' Union is probably the largest international organisation of the poorest people. If you want to get funds to where they will be most useful, why not by-pass the big organisations and the official churches, and get some buying-power into the hands of those who have least? The Mothers' Union would be ideally placed to be such a channel.

The Welsh priest and theologian Manon Ceridwen James has found women of the same kind of lineaments in rural and industrialised Wales. The 'Welsh Mam' has long been recognised as an archetype, powerful, maternal, rule-affirming. Dr James develops this kind of leadership into the image of 'The Strong

Woman', who is not necessarily maternal but who leads community resistance in a situation of poverty and disadvantage, combining a religious tradition of dissent with humour and exposure of the absurdities of status. Dr James finds this element of humour in many of the characters whom she would describe as 'Strong Women'.[27] Such a woman, eight centuries earlier, was Julian of Norwich. Just as the Miracle Plays of that era were able to take the mickey out of the pretensions of prestige, Julian could banish the devil with laughter, the laughter which pervades heaven – and, to his credit, the clergyman who came to support her was able to see the joke.[28] Humour is indeed part of our package in the struggle for truth and justice.[29]

This 'strong woman' was one picture of the relationship between male and female, derived from one kind of environment. Meanwhile, a totally different picture had been developing, over the centuries, from the 'men-only' world of Greek philosophy, followed by a major tradition of Christian celibate monasticism. Dr James has noted the tradition in western philosophy and theology, that there is really only one sex, one human norm, one default position in human being, namely the male, and that the female is derivative from and subservient to the male, 'an inferior version of the image of God'[30]. This attitude can be traced from Aristotle, through Augustine and Aquinas, and still has resonance in debates and in application, not only in ecclesiastical circles. In practice, that attitude had its place in the communities that have given us the Scriptures in both Old and New Covenants. According to the Deuteronomic wisdom, the males of God's servants may, after killing all the men on the opposite side, take the females, along with cattle, to enjoy as booty (Deuteronomy 20:14). It is hard to see this as the mandate of the same God who says that both women and men are made in God's image. But this is not the only pattern. In a thoroughly patriarchal culture, where women departed from their birth-identity and became features of their husband's household, the most ancient creation story was cherished, which reversed the pattern. It mandated the man to leave his parental background and 'cleave to his wife', making her the foundation of their new humanity (Genesis 2:24). Inconsistency! But, as I have written elsewhere in connection with the Apostle Paul, it is better to have the vision with inconsistency than to have consistency without the vision.[31]

Historically, we in Britain live with these mixed traditions. Patriarchy used to be the basis of English Law, where the wife was part of the husband's property. There is plenty of evidence of this in the history of art. If the husband saw fit, and was of sufficient status, he would pay an artist to paint a picture of his household, with himself as the embodiment of the domination system and his wife as a pretty but feeble part of the furniture. In pictures and sculptures of that genre, men's bodies may seem to have value only as dummies on which to hang opulent vesture and splendid uniforms. Of the actual person, all that we can see may be just a moustache and a couple of eyes of a man who is used to being obeyed; the rest is emblems and badges of status. For the model and for the artist, the reward for this is their affirmation of rank within the domination system.

But this is not the only message conveyed in art. In a different room in our art galleries, a visitor from Mars might get the impression that the female body is the only human form that really matters. Women's bodies are valued for themselves rather than as evidences of status. The sculpture room of the Walker Gallery in Liverpool brings you into a veritable forest of unadorned female figures; here, the artist, and the viewer, are rewarded by delight in celebrating this marvellous element in the divine Creation. Further, the image of the nursing couple is the wonderful reminder of how our individual human life came into the world; this is affirmed and celebrated further by the traditional portrayal of the Madonna, the vision of how the divine life came into the world. It is true that the creation of these images has largely been a male enterprise, but there are female artists who give their energies to the exploration of the female form. Margaret MacDonald, of the Glasgow Four (Charles Rennie Macintosh was married to her), took that exploration to a depth of boldness and intimacy and mystery which make the efforts of male artists — even her husband's — look comparatively tame and literal.

In the face of such a range of assumptions and models, let us recall the message of the Sixth Day. It states, without qualification or compromise or distinction of status, that male and female are created in the image of God. If you want to see what God is like, look at a person, any person. Further, Paul pronounced that in Christ there is no longer male and female. Female and male, we belong together in unique and equal status. Perhaps art is given to us in compensation for theology.

5.

The Climax

The Six Days Connecting to the Seventh

So we come to the Seventh Day. This is what we have been looking forward to; this is our anticipated destination. Bring out the fireworks and the fanfares!

And what do we get? Two little words. 'God rested.' Scarcely a brilliant conclusion! Anti-climax. So, do we put away the trumpets and drums?

But it is, in truth, a great moment, a brilliant arrival; we swivel around 180 degrees and change direction. The previous days have been about the past, what God had said and done in the beginning of each phase of Creation. Now we are in the present, at the Seventh Day. The Beginning is Now.

I have used the word 'terminus' to describe the function of the Seventh Day as the destination for the Six Days. That is all right as far as it goes, but it does not go far enough. 'Terminus' is where the buffers are; the journey is over. But the Seventh Day is not a stop, not a one-off event; nor, of course, are the 'makings' of the Six Days; we know that they, including ourselves, are processes, not finished products. But the Seventh Day is, especially, not a conclusion but a movement into a new programme of becoming, a new journey of promises and hopes, of efforts and trials and disappointments. For the people of the Genesis text, the Seventh Day means Sabbath. And Sabbath, as we shall see, carries a huge range of interest, of hope, of freedom. Of the Six Days, God could look and say, 'Very good'. Now we are in a world of Babylon; and, before Babylon, we are in a world controlled by Pharaoh, a world which we know is anything but very good, in fact a world which often would not seem to be God's world at all. But it is a world where God, Supreme Being, Great Creator, Almighty Power, shows that, contrary to all expectation, God is with the powerless, the loser, the people who don't matter. So the Seventh Day is a gateway to a new future, where we can feel that this is the world which we know.

As we arrive at the Seventh Day, we are in a condition that the readers of the text experience every week. The sun and the moon govern our timetables for every year, every month, and every day. The moon's phases proceed in movements of seven days; but otherwise, the natural world does not take much notice of the week. There is a secret about the week which the rest of Creation does not know. For us humans, the week is not just seven equal units of time; it is a dynamic programme; it is six plus one. That is God's special gift to us; it is grace.

Up to this point, time is about what happens to the rest of Creation. The 'day', with its division into evening and morning, affects everything else. Time controls us humans. The Seventh Day brings the blessing of the Sabbath. The Sabbath gives authority to humans to control time. It is indeed a gift and mandate from the Creator, but humans have the power to decide whether to use the gift and how to respond to the mandate.

The Sabbath has special significance for the authors and organisers of our text, the Jews. Here we find a value in the feature which I earlier suggested might be a mistake. The Seventh Day is fundamentally different from the preceding six days. It has no 'evening and morning'. It is not subject to calculation. It is the point where eternity touches into the realm of time. For eternity is what life is about when there is no measurement, when something happens for which the movement of the clock has no relevance. This is not reserved for the spiritual expert or the aesthetically privileged. Just as calculation is a function available to all humans as a function of their humanity, so is the access to that which is beyond the scope of calculation – the 'out-of-time-ness' of sexual touch, of the sight of one's first-born, of the special moment of hearing or vision. We know what it is, when we cannot put it into words. 'Jacob served seven years for Rachel, and they seemed to him but a few days because of the love he had for her' (Genesis 29:20). We know what that means; measurement is irrelevant. This is the difference between clock-time and lovers'-time, between the measured and the eternal. It is at moments of this kind that we feel most human, and that to be human is wonderful, a privilege, making life worth-while. Whether we are aware of it or not, whether we find this language helpful or not, this is where we are closest to knowing that we are made in the image of God. Philip Newell quotes the ninth-century Irish theologian Eriugena: "'Just as the essence of God is invisible and incomprehensible and passes all understanding, so it is with humanity, created in God's image." What cannot be known about us is greater by far than what can be known. The deeper we delve into the mystery of our being the more we become aware of its limitless depths.'[32] In a word, we belong in eternity. And that is not a rare privilege given to some specialist souls; it is what it means to be human. For Christians, this is finally affirmed in the one who is God taking flesh, being nailed to a cross, on a certain Friday afternoon when Pontius Pilate was Governor; that event in time made marks on his hands which he carries into eternity. Any process which treats human beings as expendable rubbish is not just bad politics; it is blasphemy. If we know that much about God, it is enough.

For the greater part of our lives, calculation and measurement are both necessary and valuable; they may even be enjoyable. But they have their limitation. Eternity is not only beyond death. Eternity is now, when we know being without measurement. To recognise eternity is, in effect, to recognise God. For God is the one who is beyond measurement, and for humans what is beyond measurement is what cannot be fully known. Theology is talk about God; of all forms of knowledge it is the one which is fundamentally and essentially inadequate. What can be said about God is necessarily less than what cannot be said. We can see something of this in sculpture, which is an art where that which is produced cannot all be seen at once. To see it, you have to move, in time, from what you can see to what you cannot see. Epstein's great statue of Jacob wrestling with the Angel is wonderfully detailed at the front and sides, and photos are often made of it. But the photographers miss out the muscular power of the Angel's back, which is the source of the energy of the whole piece. That is the difference between a sculpture and a cardboard cut-out. God tells Moses, 'You can't see my face, but if you're careful you can watch out for my back, and be content with seeing that' (Exodus 33:23). Don't pretend that you know God if all that you have got is a cardboard cut-out. The sciences of measurement and calculation have to acknowledge that their territory has its limitations. They have the Six Days as their field of authority. But that authority has its boundaries.

David Jones was a London-Welshman, who had a profound instinct for the reality of boundaries and their identity. He summarises our human areas of occupation with characteristic succinctness: 'Man is a "borderer", the sole inhabitant of a tract of country where matter marches with spirit.'[33] He recognises the same development which Dr Jenifer Baker was observing,[34] of how the early humans gained some degree of power over other creatures, animate and inanimate, by the use of tools, and then, through 'art', extended their domain not only over matter but also over spirit. In due course, humans discovered things which have no existence in the material world, such as nations, and finance, and beauty, and guilt, and heaven; and they could manipulate such things, either for co-operation or for dominance and destruction. So, as human beings, we belong in two universes. We are hybrids, depending on two sources of energy and movement which are distinct but which depend on each other and interact with each other. More than any artist since William Blake, Jones explored the interfaces between the worlds of poetry and of graphic art, with calligraphy included as an extra discipline overlapping them. Ingeniously he speaks of the 'march' together of the two territories of human being. In the 'Marches' of Wales and England, which the Welsh call *y Gororau*, and of those of Scotland, we see how we can indeed belong in more than one world.

Map-draughters and law-makers specify the points where two authorities butt up against each other; they make their definitions. But these definitions are not the whole truth. We who live in the borderlands live with all sorts of odd effects of the boundaries.[35] In practice, we know that the River Ceiriog, for all its symbolic status, does not tell us all that we need to know about who we are and where. We live in the overlapping of the authorities.

But while, in these days, we can treat these borders as interesting features from the past, we should not forget that they also stand for exclusion, anxiety, and destructiveness, both from the past and in corporate memory. Wat's Dyke is less than half a mile from where I live, and Offa's Dyke only a short way further off. They are interesting lines on the map today, but in former centuries they stood for restriction and death, the obstruction of connection. As Grahame Davies sees, a border can stand for 'no exit'; it can cause the disintegration of families, as at the border which separates North Korea from South. It can make movement hazardous or impossible, as at Calais, or at the line between Turkey and Greece, or between the USA and Mexico. It can stand for the arbitrariness of control, the uncertainty of whether the border happens to be open today or not. It can give unreliable powers to minor officials at border-posts, who can make up the rules according to their whim, as we sometimes found on the border between South Africa and what was called Rhodesia; or it can enable one to take a breath of fresh air, as we enjoyed in crossing from South Africa into eSwatini/Swaziland or Lesotho. Or, if we so choose to be irresponsible, we can treat the whole border question as insignificant, as did so many citizens east of the Irish Sea during the Brexit arguments, who just did not bother about the supremely important issue of the Irish border. The border, therefore, is not a material reality; its existence depends on human identification and power and convenience. During the Cold War period, we used to celebrate the fact that pigeons took no notice of the Berlin Wall. Now we recognise that the coronavirus similarly is not restricted by our international boundaries. Indeed, this uncertainty about identity can make a border seem to be like a virus, which can be regarded as a non-living entity, when it is not in a host, or as a living thing, capable of replicating itself, when it is located in a host. At the time when I am writing this, there is unprecedented anxiety across the world because of our uncertainty about how best to respond to the coronavirus. The answer to so many questions is, We don't know. And so, scientists and governments and ordinary citizens are burdened with the characteristic anxiety which asks, as we ask of any experiment at connection, Will it work?

The coronavirus pandemic of 2020 made us isolate ourselves from each other. Our personal 'border' took a new meaning. Grahame Davies' lines, quoted on our title-page, tell us that 'the border can release you or confine'. Hitherto, I have assumed that 'release' is good and 'confine' is bad. That interpretation is probably caused by the fact that, right from the time when my school was evacuated from my Merseyside home area to mid-Wales, I have been a lifelong border-crosser. But now I am 'confined' to a space about 50 metres by 29, half of which space is occupied by our bungalow and half by a little garden. And I recognise that this is home, safety, and protection. The border becomes precious; it enables necessary social distancing.

At this point, it may be helpful if we distinguish two kinds of people; this is the distinction between the 'local' and the 'cosmopolitan', which can be at least as significant as that of gender. It is a distinction which runs deeply through society, not least through the church. I cannot get away from the fact that I am inescapably 'cosmopolitan'; this can account for my strong emotional commitment to 'Remain' and my acute sense of loss when 'Leave' won. This border can cause deep division and misunderstanding. Across the world, what is commonly called 'culture' is defined by the 'cosmopolitan' tribe, leaving the 'local' people feeling second-class, or belonging to the nation which lost. Most of us clergy have been shaped to be 'cosmopolitans'; many Readers and Churchwardens, especially in the countryside, are 'local' people. In the New Testament, the two most powerful minds represent these two genres. Jesus of Nazareth was as local as could be. His short journey to Jerusalem was a move into a territory where politics and accents were very different from those of Galilee. Saul of Tarsus, St Paul, Greek-speaking Jewish Roman citizen, could take his cosmopolitan identity for granted. Their fundamental message was the same, but the details and references were drawn from what their life-experiences had made them. I realised something of this when I started to work in rural communities in Wales. We value the great themes of theology in different ways; creation, incarnation, spirit, trinity, salvation, baptism, church, hope – they have different values and resonances according to this distinction. And especially the clergy, shaped as we are by our professional formation, may find it difficult to speak with true sympathy to people whose great grandparents are buried in their local church's graveyard. When we had meetings of clergy and readers together, I used to ask members to get together in two groups. Group 'A' would be those who had stayed in one place and taken several different jobs or roles. Group 'B' would be those who had moved from place to place following their trade or profession. Then, in these groups, we would consider how some of the great theological elements of Gospel speak to us, how we, deep down, value something like 'baptism' or 'salvation'. When we finally came together to compare our perceptions, the differences could be quite striking.[36] For those of us who take for granted that we are cosmopolitan the coronavirus experience of 'confining' (or 'defining') can be an opening of mind and heart and sympathy.

Just as a geographical boundary, like the Berlin Wall, can be porous, so can a historical boundary, not just in big-scale political factors but also in hidden personal matters. The last major international 'plague' to affect Britain was the so-called 'Spanish flu', in 1918–19, which claimed the lives of 228,000 people in this country. My father, as I mentioned before, was with the Army in France for two years from 1917. Early in 1919 he returned to Cheshire, to find that his wife and infant son had died in the flu. Six years later, aged 45, he married again. In 1927, his wife, then aged 39, gave birth to me. If the flu had not happened, I would never have come into existence; the two unique genetic inheritances which make me me would never have come together. And you, a hundred years after that pandemic, would not, at this moment, be reading this text. Now, there may well be something much more deserving of your attention; but we can just note that a century is not necessarily a boundary in history, and I am left with the question: if I owe my existence to the 1919 pandemic, when might be the effect of the 2020 version?

As borderers, we can recognise, in many departments of life, the ways in which boundaries work for us, or don't work for us. Whatever the clocks may tell us, we know that there is only a gradual change from 11:55 to 12:05. Dawn and twilight are times of special meaning – and, on the road in these days, special danger. There is only a gradual change from Winter to Spring (that is one of the blessings of our British climate – in South Africa there is nothing like the gradualness which blesses Britain in the changes of the seasons; there, we in effect had only summer and winter). Without the wetlands and seashore and mudflats all sorts of creatures would have no existence. Our friends in Yorkshire might complain that it's neither nowt nor summat; but hybrid landscape is essential in the total web which nourishes us.

When I took responsibility for a small missionary training college, we needed to update the library. We found that most of the books recommended for our students, and, indeed, most of the interesting books on the market just did not fit into the categories in the catalogues. New categories were required, for studies which were at the interface of politics and sociology, between science and faith, between ethics and economics. These were the books that made connections; they were the border-puncturers. Boundaries were necessary, but across existing categories. At the same time, it's not all just a vague blur. There are points of critical change – 'tipping-points'. There are critical points. There comes a point in the bending of a spring where the load is such that the piece fails to return to its original shape; excessive stress results in strain – something which we see in the lives of organisations and of individual persons.

The whole notion of classification originates in the naming of the 'days'. There is indeed a definable boundary between the world of the Six Days and the world of the Seventh. But there is also a profound overlap. As we have seen, the world of matter and of measurement carries with it the implications for the spiritual obedience of humans towards the world of matter. And, as we get into our exploration of the Seventh Day, we shall see that its spiritual identity has vital implications for our living in the world of matter and of calculation. Our role as borderers is to recognise these identities and work for the proper interaction of their territories.

There are places where the boundary between matter and spirit is very slight. George MacLeod, the founder of the Iona Community, used to say that the Island of Iona is 'a thin place', a place where the boundary is transparent.[37] It's easy enough to see that it is beautiful and tranquil – even though, when I have been there, it has usually been a place of hard work and demanding encounters. But as well as its natural beauty there is, in the tantalising words of Hendrik Willem van Loon which I have already quoted, 'plus something else'. And I suggest that the 'something else' is derived from the Community's other basic root in the world, the 'thick' boundaries of the big city's places of oppression, deprivation, and loss. The original motive for the Community lay, as it still does, in the claims of the poorest areas of Glasgow. Without that fundamental purpose, God would not have allowed the Community to flourish. The same is true of that other gift of God of the twentieth century, Taizé. It is valued for the 'Taizé style' of worship which it has shared. But it would not have been allowed to exist as a source of spiritual delight if it were not fundamentally committed to its original motive, of being an agency for the healing of the international and inter-tribal fractures that have been destroying Europe for so many recent generations. Where the borders have been 'thick', both these movements have filed away at them, and have generated a degree of 'thin-ness'.

The borderland of matter and spirit can occur in all sorts of places. I was called up into the RAF on the last day of World War II, as an Airframe Fitter. I was posted to a station on the Welsh-English border. There, as I have already mentioned, there were hundreds of redundant aircraft parked on the grass, brand-new, but surplus to requirements. Our job was to rescue some of these decaying aircraft, mostly heavy bombers, from the scrap yard; we were to make them serviceable, to fly off and to do what bombers do. Many of them had been built in the adjoining factory, which is still building aircraft to this day. While we were renovating these weapons of destruction, the factory was very busy. It was not producing more bombers. Its equipment, its materials, its skilled workers, its financial resource, its transport system, its admin, had been converted for the production of 28,000 prefabricated bungalows, to provide housing in the worst-damaged areas of the country. All the matter-stuff was retained, but diverted into a new spirit of enterprise. It was the nearest thing that I have known to the vision of 'swords into ploughshares'. I think that it is most unlikely that any of the very modern machines that I was working on still exist. But there are people still living in those bungalows.

The transition from the Sixth Day to the Seventh is the transition between our human identity as matter and our human identity as spirit. The Seventh Day takes us into the world of spirit, the environment of eternity. That is the mercy of the Seventh Day. The world in all its measurable complexity was in business; the process for its creation had been set in motion. What was missing was what cannot be measured. The shorthand name for that is 'rest'. On the Seventh Day the Creator created rest.

> 'Throughout the week, we work to utilise the world around us for its godly purpose; on the Sabbath, all the worlds, from the lowest to the highest, elevate upwards. They all strive to be closer to the divine. That is why the story of the Sabbath in the Torah occupies a different chapter, because it is entirely different and higher than the rest of the week.'[38]

So this validates the break in the flow of the chapter after the Sixth Day. The Seventh Day is not merely a space at the end of the six, nor is it just a neat conclusion. It is the day which gives shape and meaning and authority to the whole week. It is the signature of the Maker upon all that has been made. As we shall see, the symbol of Sabbath came to carry a great cargo of meaning for the Hebrew people, touching every side of life and law. So there is some justification for the creation of Sabbath to start a new chapter in the story. It might be appropriate for the Seventh Day to have a short but distinct chapter on its own. But, unfortunately, as printed nowadays, it appears to be merely tacked on to the beginning of the Adam and Eve story, which is a totally different piece of writing.

We shall be noting some of the range of meanings that Sabbath came to carry for God's People. But first we need to reckon with its primary meaning, its meaning for God. It is what it is because of what it is for God. God rests. For the Six Days, God has been doing, giving things their mandate to be. In the Seventh Day, God rests from Doing. The Seventh Day is when God is free to Be. God is Creator; but God is not totally defined by that function. God is the One who is. God Creator gives Godself freedom to be. That freedom is the source and the motive for all our liberation. The liberation of Israel in Egypt, the freedom of the oppressed exiles in Babylon, the freedom which, as we shall see, God enables by intervention in the fatalisms of economic and social forces, the freedom by which Jesus defies the narrowness and the criticism of the authorities of the law, all these expressions of freedom are mirrors of God's freedom, of God's refusal to be tied down by the categories with which our limited human intelligence may seek to restrict and define. God is simply free. 'God wills what he knows and loves, God loves what he knows and wills, God knows what he wills and loves. That is his freedom.'[39] That simple freedom is what God Creator shares with us, enabling us to defy the limitedness and the exclusion with which the systems of control and fear can trap us. That is Sabbath.

Christians rejoice to accept the blessing of the Sabbath and to recognise it as Sunday. For Jews and Christians alike, that blessing is there for us, because this is what God is like. God rests, and we rest.[40] The Babylonian divinities also rest; but their human underlings do not rest; they have to continue in their menial tasks, serving the gods. The God of the Hebrews rests, and because humans are made in God's image, they are like God; they also rest. It is part of our design, our normality.

But, where do we find the 'normal' human being? Dentistry can show us what a normal set of teeth — as opposed to an average set of teeth — is like; but, a 'normal' person? Frank Lake, in his *Clinical Theology*, refers to Aristotle's remark that if we want to examine what is normal we must be careful that we are examining unspoiled specimens of the species.[41] And he goes on to quote Martin Niemöller's aphorism, which we ourselves heard from its author on his visit to South Africa: 'Jesus Christ is human, we are not.'[42] This recalls Martin Luther's description of Jesus as 'the Proper Man'. In Jesus we do have a specimen of what 'normal' humanity is like. And we have to acknowledge, on the evidence of his story, that conventional human 'normality' rejects and crucifies this true normality. But in the story of Jesus we are given sufficient sight of the lineaments and the architecture of such true normality. It is not a matter of a particular selection of personality traits. It is a normality based on relationship with the eternal. From evidence in the Gospels, especially that according to St John, Lake derives a quadrilateral cycle of four movements, traced by the Son in relationship with the Father. I offer now a simplified adaptation of Lake's diagram.

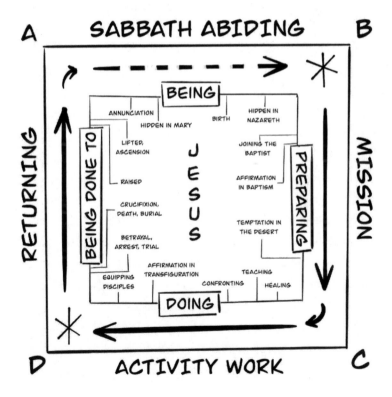

The movement 'A to B' represents Belonging, or Abiding. The Father starts the process by sending the angel to Mary, announcing the coming of the Son into the world via a human mother, in whose body the Son is hidden for nine months; then in her household he is hidden for about thirty years. He is controlled by Nazareth's timetable, simply Being, Belonging, being Accepted. Then at B, he moves out in Mission; he finds that there are several groups that are offering solutions to the nation's problems but he chooses John Baptist, who speaks and lives like a prophet of the old type. He accepts his baptism, there he is Affirmed, his Mission and his Status are announced. His first move is into the desert, alone. He has to discover who he is and what God's Word has to say about his mandates. Then at C, he starts to Do, to Achieve, taking charge of his own programme, working, teaching, forming a community, opposing the powers of evil. He fulfils the mission of Messiah but goes beyond the expectations of convention. This active public presence of the Son in the world is a wonderful blessing, but it does not go on indefinitely. There is a further Affirmation (towards point D), on the mountain-top, where earth and heaven overlap, and he speaks with other persons, beyond history, about his 'exodus'. From this point, he has a more limited mandate; his face is set towards Jerusalem. He goes on teaching, but with a more limited agenda and a more limited public, the disciple-group. He arrives at the Holy City and its Temple. He equips his disciples, makes them sharers in the sacrifice of his body and blood. He prepares them for the Spirit's coming to them to enable them to be his continuing body. He lets them overhear his conversation with the Father. From this point, his Doing reduces and his Being-done-to predominates – being prostrated by dread and uncertainty, being controlled by other people's timing, being betrayed, arrested, deserted, denied, treated as rubbish, being crucified, being raised from death, being lifted to heaven in Returning to the Father, for a further life of Abiding.[43]

Christ shows us human normality, humanity as it is designed to be. As members of the Body of Christ, we may be able to see some of this process in our own experience. We do not start it ourselves – our origin is in being created and cherished by God, in whom we can abide from our beginning. We are affirmed and identified in our baptism. We celebrate this when we meet in the fellowship of the Church, and we do not just drift off afterwards, we are sent with a mission into the world. We get on with our Activity and our Achievement, which may feel like failure; it may involve being crucified, but it is still made possible by the previous Abiding. Our Activity is not indefinite. There comes a point, which we may resist or regret, when we withdraw from Activity, like Jesus – going up a mountain, rising before dawn, or staying in our room. We prepare for the new meeting with the Father, the Creator; this may be short, like our preparation for weekly meeting at the Sacrament, or it may last for a whole Lent. Then we find the Acceptance, but our Acceptance is not a reward for successful Activity; it is the persistent love of the Creator. We accept this Acceptance, as it affirms that our Abiding is the eternal truth about us.

This is my own understanding of Lake's original exposition, and it may not exactly follow his specification. But I think that it works and is true to the Gospel. This four-stage pattern is, I suggest, more realistic and more fruitful than a simple 'coming and going' pattern which is often offered as a spiritual discipline. As Dr Lake used to suggest, it follows neatly the parable of our blood-circulation; our blood is renewed as it 'rests' in our lungs, then it goes out along our arteries to love the tissues as it has itself been loved in the lung, then, before it is exhausted, it returns to be renewed. It belongs. This fits with the Genesis pattern, where morning follows evening, activity follows sleep; and achievement follows abiding. 'The energy and creativity of the day emerge from the dark stillness of the night. If we are to be creative in the day we must first give ourselves to the stillness of the night.'[44]

As we shall come to see, the fulfilment of 'Sabbath' involves a lot of obedient and planned activity. But it is activity designed to enable and to share 'shalom', the state of peace and justice which is the 'normality' of our Creator's intention. How far this can be achieved will not depend on our cleverness or personal ambition or on our particular bundle of personality traits; it will depend on the quality of our 'abiding', in the rest and renewal which are the basis of Sabbath.

6.

The Seventh Day

Connecting to Labour

The mandate of the Sixth Day has been about our responsibilities and duties, as workers together with our Creator. We are designed to work. There should be scope for everyone's contribution. It is a cruel deception when we claim an increase in productivity simply by reducing the numbers of those engaged in production, and by increasing the numbers of those excluded – the poorest, the disabled, the homeless, the unemployed.

In our employment, we are required to make decisions and choices, to exercise effort and skill. This will mean differences of role and of activity, along with differences of levels of decision-making. This may lead to differences of status and of reward. But such differences have boundaries. The mandate of the Seventh Day intervenes. For one day in every seven, the differences between employer, employee, and unemployed are cancelled. For 14 per cent of our time, we are set free from work-roles and classifications. We are equal in the presence of God. This is why the story of Creation is compressed into six 'days'. If it were expressed as, say, six periods of five million years each, that would have no connection with our own experience of time. A five-million-year period of rest after every thirty million years would be meaningless. The story of Creation is told so as to have real significance for our handling of time, and for our organisation of work. It gives the highest possible authority for the blessings and the sanctions of the Sabbath, the Seventh Day. It gives us the motive for our weekly thanksgiving for our work, whatever it is, and for our non-work, for the fact that we are released from slavery. Perhaps it is true, as Prime Minister Harold Wilson is reputed to have said, that a week is a long time in politics. But, for many of us, it is a blessedly short time. Whether it is for the weekly chore of putting out the rubbish for recycling, or for the Saturday night out, seven days can pass wonderfully fast. Let us be thankful for this routine interruption.

Our common understanding of the Sabbath laws is that they are mainly about worship. Indeed, the Sabbath, and the Christian Sunday, are about our freedom to be equal in the presence of God, to share equally in the bread that God gives with equal value to each of us. But first of all, Sabbath law is a labour law. It celebrates that we are delivered from slavery (Deuteronomy 5:15). We are more than our market value. We are not defined only by our work-label. We are not measured only by our achievements, our level in economic competition, or our success in fulfilling targets set for us by a system which tells us who we are. We are, in a word, redeemed. 'Redemption' is an economic term; to be redeemed is to be delivered from slavery, no longer just a thing measured by the arithmetic of the market.

Slavery is not far away from us in Britain. It is there in our recent history, in one way or another. Many of us live in cities whose wealth was based in the slave trade. Others of us come from families whose members, only a few generations ago, were slaves. In South Africa, I had colleagues whose grandparents, within living memory, had been slaves. It is claimed that there are 40.3 million slaves in the world now, more than ever before, 136,000 in the UK.[45] In the past, people became slaves through being born into slavery, or as result of conquest or capture or economic transaction. Nowadays, many people find themselves enslaved as victims of deliberate deception, of phoney promises of employment or enticing schemes of loans. For many, the main cause of their slavery is indebtedness. At international level, huge numbers of people live in nations which still have to pay interest on debts of which the capital has already been repaid. The Jubilee 2000 movement has succeeded in making this scandal more widely recognised; but the indebtedness still has its toxic effects on international relationships. At an individual level, many of us in this country have had to face the mercilessness of organisations which threaten to trap us with the relentless pressures of pay-day loans. Congratulations to Archbishop Justin Welby of Canterbury, for his head-on defiance of Wonga, a typical organisation of this kind; and to the Credit Union movement which, often with church backing, aims to make responsible credit accessible where it is needed; and to those banks which, like the Co-op, treat their customers as morally responsible people who will take an interest in the bank's ethical decisions. This is genuine Sabbath observance.

So it is still true that nowhere are we far from slavery. The mandate to struggle against slavery is no optional extra; it is there at the heart of the story of our creation. The interests of the slave have priority; and that is very different from the procedures in nineteenth-century Britain, when concern for the compensation of slave-owners for their loss of investment took priority over any concern for the compensation of slaves for their loss of freedom. The Jewish Law is clear, that a released slave must be equipped with all the resources necessary for making a new start in life

(Deuteronomy 15:13). This is an example of the character of God which we shall meet again, the God of the Second Chance, which Professor John Rogerson defines as 'the imperative of redemption'.[46]

In our day, a new kind of slavery may be making its claim upon us; instead of being slaves to alien taskmasters, we make slaves of ourselves. Valuable equipment which we buy – or is provided for us – to ease the burden of work can take over our timetables and our lives. Mark Scarlata has pointed out how we have come to 'live in a restless culture that is constantly switched on'. 'Our screens are always connected and invite us into a digital world that never rests... Technology has the potential to become as oppressive as Egypt. It may be a self-imposed bondage, but digital slavery is no less destructive to the human soul than physical slavery.'[47]

The Bible is a dangerous book in a slave-owning society. Unlike the mythologies of ancient Babylon and Egypt, unlike the philosophies of Greece, the Bible's songs and stories have a positive message for slaves. It tells them, your slavery is not inevitable; freedom is possible. Even when, as in the conditions of New Testament times, most slaves were not going to get actual liberation, teachers like St Paul were doing something unheard-of elsewhere; they were treating slaves as responsible adults who could make moral decisions, as sisters and brothers in Christ. Even within the bondage of slavery, freedom was possible. Paul wrote to a church many of whose members would have been slaves, saying: 'You are free; you are where you are because in Christ you are free. That is the truest truth about you – hold to it.' There is that core of freedom inside yourself, in the redeemed human spirit, a freedom which no one can take away from us (Galatians 5:1). This is freedom of a similar style to that which

Viktor Frankl discovered within the conditions of Auschwitz.[48] We are made for freedom, the tyrants are doomed. I remember a Bible-study session, when, as we finished, some white Rhodesians said, 'We must never let our natives hear this.' In that particular context, there was officially no slavery; but people were being treated as if they were indeed slaves.

The message of the Bible has been transmitted across the centuries, and its symbols carry a rich cargo of meaning. It tells us that there is a 'Red Sea' for us to cross out of our present condition, and a 'Jordan' for us to cross into a new world. 'Jordan' remains still a boundary in the Middle East – a physical, social, and political symbol of the most intransigent of the world's troubles. But also, 'Jordan' is, for many of us, the boundary which we look forward to crossing when we die. But also again, the original singers of songs like 'Deep River, my home is over Jordan', were slaves in the southern states of the USA, yearning for an escape-route. For them 'Jordan' was the Ohio, the boundary between the southern slave-owning states and the free.

While I was writing this, an old friend and colleague telephoned to say that her husband had just died, after two years of stressful illness. They were a couple with a generous and long-standing commitment to justice and peace across the world. She enthusiastically told me that, at his funeral, they would be singing 'Guide me, O thou great Redeemer', and that for her own funeral she was arranging for the organist to give a special boost to the words:

> 'When I tread the verge of Jordan,
> Bid my anxious fears subside;
> Death of death, and hell's destruction
> Land me safe on Canaan's side.'

In reply, I mentioned the Ohio significance of 'Jordan'. It turned out that my friend knew far more about it than I. I have never travelled anywhere near the Ohio, but she had been there. She and her husband had visited a 'safe house' on that river bank, provided by sympathisers on the 'underground railroad', the dangerous route towards Canada, taken by slaves escaping from the south. She had stood in the window where the host would hold a light to tell the slaves that the coast was clear for them to come forward to make the crossing. Sometimes, they would have had to wait a long time for that light to shine; for my friend's husband, it had been two years. But, in making such a crossing, there would be a solidarity of support, a communion of saints.

You may ask, what has all that got to do with our text? What place has it in what is supposed to be an academically respectable publication? I reply: for both Jews and Christians, the Scripture is given to us not only to inform but to inspire; it is to support us in our calling to be agents of God's purposes and representatives of God's kingdom. We may try to find meaning, using our intellectual skills; but sometimes meaning finds us, through the Spirit's grace. The Scripture is doing what it is supposed to do, when it speaks to our imagination as much as it does to our intellect. The living word makes connections, for us to recognise and to be inspired by. If the purpose of our theology is merely to inform us, then a statement of doctrine will suffice. But the measure of our theology should be that it enables us to get involved with God's programme of mercy, and of justice, and of overcoming the lovelessness that mars the creation. Only if this is its purpose will it be true to its founding documents in the Scriptures. And this happens through story and song, as well as through prose and doctrine. A book like this present one is, perhaps, not going to do more than make us critical; to get us moving in the way of the Creator. We need to be inspired in our imagination, so that we begin to see ourselves as actually involved in the Creator's task. And that is why the Word became flesh, to give us the story in which we can share and the song to celebrate it. So one page of story is likely to be more useful than fifty pages of argument, in getting us motivated and in enabling us to stand up against the demons and discouragements that the world throws at us.

Many years ago, I was with a politically active friend, who had just received a short letter. It said: 'Dear Sir, I have read your manifesto with great interest, but it does not say anything about singing. Yours faithfully.' This book is not, primarily, a political manifesto; but, in this chapter and the two following, it is concerned about God's law, and, in the Hebrew Scriptures, where you have law, song is not far away. God's law is not just a lot of rules to obey but a gift from a loving Creator, to be celebrated. Typically, the longest chapter of the Bible consists of the 176 verses of Psalm 119, a long song of praise for God's law. There can be no Leviticus and Exodus without the Psalms, no Sermon on the Mount without the Magnificat of Mary. I do not have the skill to write a song for you to sing at this point; but, if you are taking these chapters seriously, it could make good sense for you to break off from reading and sing something cheerful; you could do worse than sing that familiar version of the Hundredth Psalm, 'All People that on earth do dwell' – it fits perfectly.

In this book, I am trying to make connections with theology. So I am not surprised that I am finding myself quoting from a great song of William Williams Pantecelyn. In the land of my fathers, a theology which does not include the work of singers like Pantecelyn and Ann Griffiths would not be theology. There is a very old story about a distinguished academic gentleman who had been looking forward to being confirmed; but he was backing out because he felt that he had to admit, 'I can't say the creed'. However, prompted by a quiet nudge from the Chaplain, he added, 'But I can sing it', and so he went ahead. A creed is only half a creed until it is sung.

One of the wisest people I have known was a man employed as a carpenter on the goldmine at which I was a priest as my first appointment in South Africa. He was a small-scale builder, very like Joseph father of Jesus. He was called Wynand Lee, living in the so-called 'native location', where he had built a little church and served there as Catechist. When I started to act as their priest, I was surprised to find that, apart from hymns, they were not used to singing the congregational parts of the Mass. I asked Mr Lee for his advice. He replied, 'If you sing parts like the Gloria and Creed, you cut out those who can't sing (in fact, about 0.5 per cent of the congregation). If you don't sing, you cut out those who can't read (about 50 per cent). If you sing, those who can't read will pick up the words by ear, and if they can't do that they will sing la la la, and that will be their worship and God will hear it and understand.' So we sang! There was a Mass-setting, used all over South Africa, based on chants which could easily fit all our languages, so that, especially in town churches, we could sing together in half-a-dozen languages at the same time – truly Pentecost. Mr Lee himself (as a 'coloured' man, with his family, where Mrs Lee was midwife to virtually everyone in the 'location') was Afrikaans-speaking at home; but he was fluent in both English and Zulu, like many of our catechists, and so was a Pentecost in person.

For many of us, the greatest loss in the pandemic lockdown, second only to our inability to meet friends at the Sacrament, was the lack of singing. We were warned that singing is dangerous for passing infection. Indeed, singing is infectious, in more ways than one. It can communicate our awareness of God in a way that is missed by mere books. Singing can, we should confess, be dangerous for spreading and encouraging dangerous nonsense, nationalistic hatred, and historic untruths. The second verse of God Save the Queen (scatter our enemies, frustrate their knavish tricks, etc) is still printed in hymnbooks that I have used for much of my life. We can find ourselves singing things which we would not dream of saying in prose. Theology must watch critically over its expressions. But that does not invalidate the creative value of our song. In our gatherings of students during the apartheid years in South Africa, what many of us remember best is the community of song. In music, we found, on the whole, that the high priests of the classical tradition had little to say to our situation, and the conventional songs of the pop scene also passed by on the other side. But new ground had been prepared for us by the emergence of Johannesburg Township Jazz, marrying a distinct ancestry of New Orleans with a unique urban African voice of social poignancy. Now, in the 1960s, what spoke to us was the contribution of the folk singers of the Civil Rights struggle – like Pete Seeger, with Bob Dylan's 'A Hard Rain's A-Gonna Fall', spelling out the surprises and costs of the struggle, in symbolic terms which could almost be the dialogue between the Father and the Son on the Mount of the Transfiguration; like Joan Baez, lamenting where all the flowers had gone, with a voice of bell-like purity with which she was still able to captivate us forty years later, in person, at the International Eisteddfod. This was infectious – along with the songs of our own nations, such as Tshotsholoza, and Nkosi Sikelel, the singing of which was against the law. Many of these South African songs found their way into the Iona Community's Wild Goose Worship collection, 'Freedom is Coming'.

In 2002, at the International Eisteddfod in Llangollen, we found all our standards were being overturned by an amazing choir, called Stellenberg or Pro Cantu, based in a depressed area of the Western Cape of South Africa, led by an extraordinary conductor, André van der Merwe. They just swept the board with the quality and variety of their songs. They won almost every competition which they entered. As a choir, they had been in existence for only five years. They were all young people from local schools and colleges, of every race-group in the country. This choir could not have existed under the previous regime. If anyone asks, 'what was wrong with apartheid?', I would answer, 'Look at that choir; apartheid made such a choir impossible; that is why apartheid had to be destroyed.' Among many other items, they sang the Afro-American spirituals from Michael Tippett's powerful oratorio 'A Child of Our Time' – itself a creative protest against the domination systems that crucify the hidden people. Their account of 'Deep River, my home is over Jordan' is as true and authoritative as any could be. There will be some critics who say – just as there are historians who say similar of the Confessing Church in Germany under the Hitler regime – that these sort of contributions are not worth noticing, for they are politically impotent. Well, such songs and such singers may not get into the academic reading-lists, but they pass the infection of wisdom in ways that go beyond the power of prose. And the Kingdom of God scores.

But there is another cautionary flag which we must raise, amid all this delight in song. In Llangollen, and not only in Llangollen, I have heard sermons and speeches about the power and beauty of music which imply that people who cannot hear the music are automatically to be reckoned as incomplete adults or second-class citizens. It is deeply true that Black People Matter, and that is a theme which rightly has claimed our commitment and dedication. But, equally, Deaf People Matter. Exclusion stands against them, not unlike the exclusion created by racism. In Wales, both the International and the National Eisteddfodau are committed to policies of inclusion. Deaf people find in corporate sign-language events the same sense of togetherness and artistry that choral singers value. Jesus was certainly Deaf-Aware. His followers are mandated to practice inclusion as he himself did. recognising the method and integrity of all cultures of communication, including those of the Deaf communities (Mark 7:31–37).

The Scriptures bring to us the song and the story of the symbol of 'Jordan'. As we have seen, this tells us that our preparation for our own individual death is totally tied up with our commitment to work for the elimination of slavery, to support the movement of freedom wherever it may take us. We are called to help to make Exodus real in our own day. Even for the slave, there is an alternative citizenship, in the purpose of the Creator. This is part of the witness of the Seventh Day; our mandate is to remember that we were slaves, and that therefore there should be a regular interruption of labour-relationships. As with the other commandments, the fourth commandment is an integral part of our createdness. It insists that, even if you are a slave-owner, that is true for only six days out of every seven, for you and your slave alike. Remember that you are a liberated slave yourself, and therefore the Sabbath is the continuing truth about you (Deuteronomy 5:15). A doctrine of Creation which does not affirm the rights of labour is a defective doctrine; its believers have to be reminded that the Sabbath is its unfinished business.

The Sabbath, the Seventh Day, stands as a structure of interruption, a break in the otherwise relentless dominance of earning and payment, of economic control and ownership. That interruption is deliverance; it is mercy. That mercy stands as critic and encourager in much of our public life. For instance, we can all say that 'We love the NHS'. But, as Bishop Lesslie Newbigin pointed out over thirty years ago, 'A Welfare State operating on the principle that I am my brother's keeper cannot be permanently maintained on the basis of an economy operating on the principle that I am not.'[49] As one who has recently benefitted unexpectedly and deeply from the ministrations of the National Health Service, I feel this issue very sharply. Archbishop Welby identifies 'the capital of capitalism, the commercial hub of the world' as 'Babylon'.[50] Newbigin's contention could be expressed as: can Babylon maintain the NHS? Can Babylon submit to the mandates of Sabbath? A mixed economy supposes that it is not impossible. A crisis such as the COVID-19 pandemic is causing a Conservative Government to behave in ways which look unfamiliar and contrary to its conventional instincts. In the longer run, which way will get the priority in the heart of the Great British Public?

For many committed people, including earnest Christians, we do not have to look far to identify the slave-owner. It is ourself. We can be auto-slaves, under compulsion of our own self-image, our own target of success, our own resistance to failure. We cannot let go. And we enslave others. We have to have failures around us, to assure us of our own successful identity. We have to have someone to oppose, whose faults can nourish us. We co-opt others into our own search for superiority, and thus become enslavers ourselves (Galatians 6:4). That also can be corporate. We have to have the church that we don't go to, whose short-comings can reinforce our soundness. We, in some manner, pay them to be wrong. (There was value in the old ecumenical proverb: Christians are usually right in what they affirm and wrong in what they deny.) All this is especially dangerous for God-fearing people. We may know the kind of layworker for whom the return to secular work on Monday provides welcome respite from the demands of Sunday. We are servants of God, and God, being infinite, can make infinite demands on us. So we can make God our slave-owner, living, in Milton's terrible phrase, always 'in the great Task-Master's eye'.[51] Such a god is no better than Orwell's Big Brother, or the East German Stasi, or our old foe BOSS, the South African Bureau for State Security, who always had an Informer sitting close to us. But Sabbath is the gift of the God of Exodus, the Liberator, whom the Hebrew people could affirm and rely on even in the oppression of Babylon. That God, whose yoke is easy, can deliver us even from ourselves. In our attempts to be obedient to the Supreme Lord, we remember that the Lord's commandment is that we should rest, genuinely physically and mentally rest; and that we take responsibility for enabling others to rest, including the aliens and migrants and sojourners among us. It's all there in the fourth commandment, and in the gift of the Seventh Day. God rests; in God's image and likeness, we rest.

God remains the Creator, God rests, but that does not mean that God ceases to work. And all this concern about resting, and all our commitment to abolish slavery, these do not mean that work is the enemy. The Sabbath rest is a judgement on work: but it is also the blessing of work. There was a popular hymn which celebrated 'those endless Sabbaths the blessed ones see' – which made some lively people protest that if heaven was endless Sabbath, they would get tickets for the other place. Whatever may be true of heaven, that's not our problem; on earth, endless is what the Sabbath definitely is not. Sabbath is a regular and limited interruption, not an abolition of work. It is a pause, when we can stand back and reflect on our work, to offer our commitment and imagination and energy and activity. The Bible does not lead us to despise, or merely to put up with, the claims of work. There is not room here to list the various kinds of workers that the Bible mentions — everything from the sons of Adam with their agricultural responsibilities to Jesus of Nazareth, carpenter, botanist and student of political economy (Jesus, as a 'carpenter', which means a small-scale builder, would be familiar with local conditions of land-tenure and ownership); and there was Paul, tent-maker, weather-forecaster, and employer of secretaries, along with a continual flow of home-makers, of parents and other people involved in the birth, nurture, and education of children, of administrators and politicians, and a great range of craft-workers for town and Temple, in making and building, repairing and maintaining. A list of the trades mentioned in the Bible would fill many pages. For all this, the Sabbath can be a dedication.

As a priest, I have tried to encourage people to make an offering of their work, in one way or another, at the Offering at the Eucharist. Every Sunday can be a little Harvest Festival, with the implications of Deuteronomy 26. Indeed, the Harvest Festival itself can be a valuable celebration of our work. Some clergy find it a bore; but, when I was last a parish priest, there were annually thirteen Harvest Festival services altogether in the group, including both the English and the Welsh, and I was amazed and delighted by the variety. Each place had its own character. But the trouble is that the event, which should be a celebration of the variety of work, has too often degenerated into a display of pretty things. A real Harvest Festival needs to be planned well in advance, with an open invitation to all the people of the area to bring the signs and the products of their work. It can include a 'creed' of people's work. A printed list of all the occupations followed by members, saying, in effect, 'I believe in the work that I do, I see its place — however small, however unappealing, in

God's world.' This is the implication of Deuteronomy 26, which is rightly seen as the most appropriate passage of scripture for the purpose; we should note how, if we read the whole chapter, that the celebration is for the benefit of the poor, the stranger, the migrant, the easily-forgotten. The box for the foodbank has its vital place. So does our place within a world-wide exchange of commerce and nourishment. And it involves testimony, someone telling the story of the Creator's faithfulness. And it may be right to leave a space empty, to represent the offering which the unemployed or disabled cannot make – although often it is just those kind of people who come up with most interesting offerings. The virtue of that kind of celebration can overflow into the offertory of every Sunday's Eucharist.

For some, it may be easier than for others, to see how their work can be an offering to the Creator. The goldmine at which (in addition to about fifteen out-stations, in a very rural area sixty miles by ninety) I was a priest on my first appointment in South Africa employed about three thousand people, mainly African men, who came from all over southern and central Africa. Gold-mining involves digging a hole many thousands of feet deep into the earth, with huge expenditure of energy, human and environmental, often leaving the earth dangerously unstable, then extracting from what is dug up a tiny percentage of ore, making a still tinier percentage of this into actual gold things, and finally turning the rest into ingots, to take across the Atlantic to bury in more deep holes at Fort Knox. How do you make an intelligent offering to God of that sort of work? At one stage of history, this enterprise was good for stabilising the world's economic system. Whether that still applies, I leave it to the economists to tell us. But the human skills, of co-operation, courage, and energy are there to be offered, taken into worship and dedication; somehow

81

the Creator can claim and bless even this sort of confused and compromised enterprise, while at the same time laying against it the critique and limitation represented by the Sabbath.

But there are various groups of people for whom the whole idea of regular work, and therefore regular rest, is not part of their world. There are, for instance, those parasites on the working world, beloved of a certain genre of novelists, who are called 'gentlemen of independent means', with, of course, their attendant ladies. This is the state of life to which the privileged élite of Babylonian and Roman empires aspired, and has been sought by empire-builders ever since. In fact, they are more dependent than anyone, dependent for everything on the wealth and products generated by the energies of others. At the other end of the system, there are those who are, for whatever reason, permanently 'out of work', people who, in spite of their persistent endeavours, just cannot find an employer to take them on. Some of them are blocked by disabilities which make employers look elsewhere. In former days, Local Authorities could try to be helpful and just, providing social workers to support people with disabilities, offering advisors and intermediaries concerning employment. These were trained, experienced, and accountable to the public authority. But 'austerity' has hit those who most need such support; instead, we have a proliferation of agencies, consultatives, and advisors, operatives who may be self-appointed, inexperienced, unaccountable, whose main efforts seem to be directed at organising useless interviews. A Sabbath-directed community will recognise that for there to be rest from work there has to be work to rest from. To be unemployed means to be excluded from the community of shared responsibility and of shared rest.

And then there is the great spread of people like me, the pensioners. We don't 'work', we don't clock on and off; are we also outside the community of Sabbath? For some, this is painfully true; for some, retirement from work is an end of meaning and of being valued. For others, retirement is a blessing, a release, when we can stuff a filthy uniform into the dustbin and come home using the front door and begin a new life. We pensioners are not a drain on resources – we are sustained by being paid a wage which has been put on one side for us over many years. We are free to organise our own Sabbath-pattern. Without us, a huge enterprise of voluntary work, in church and in the rest of society, would grind to a halt. We know that we are not in control of our lives; the date of our death is not inscribed in our diary, but it is the next certain event for us. We are doing less and we are being done-to more. But that is part of the package as we approach the River. Within a narrowing world we may be freer than we were when we were monitored by the firm's time-schedule or even by the church's clock.

This book is a pensioner's signing-off. It may appear to be designed to follow an orderly pattern, with a subject-matter consciously organised and fitted to size. But it's not been like that in practice. What is printed as the final chapter – which is indeed the message that most excites and inspires me – was written about three years ago, when I was only 90. The sentences that I am writing now appear in the middle of the published text; but they are in fact the last paragraph that I intend to write, and this is in some ways the part about which I am most ignorant. My writing has come in phases, in times of enlightenment and times of confusion. In that sense it is timed; it has known the constraints and the freedom of Sabbath. At the end of the day, I click on 'sign out'. In reply, a Sabbath-message appears on the screen: 'Monitor is going to sleep.'

Amen. So be it.

7.

The Seventh Day

Connecting to Land

The Sabbath law, in the Hebrew Scriptures, applies not only to labour but also to the structures of wealth as a whole, and most especially to that element which, more even than gold, underlies our wealth-system, namely the land.

My ministry in South Africa started in 1956. At that time, there was quite a strong sense among liberal-minded people that the evil of racial segregation was fundamentally a matter of ignorance and prejudice, which could be overcome by prayer and education. But, as the apartheid system screwed its increasingly unjust tentacles into every facet of life, that diagnosis came to seem inadequate. As I got to know African colleagues as friends, I came to recognise that, beyond the inequalities in education, beyond the interference of racist legislation into every aspect of personal and family life, beyond the injustice of job-reservation, and the destruction of the last vestiges of democratic rights for black people, there was an underlying evil which caused the deepest anger. This was the knowledge that the land itself had been stolen from them.

Traditionally, the land was, for Africans, the property of the tribe, or of the chief, holding it on behalf of the community. Individuals could sell or buy the right to use or work the land, they could sell the usufruct, the product of their work, but they could not sell or buy the land itself. You could no more own the land than you could own the air. But colonial powers came, including Christian missions, and engaged in transactions which, in their understanding, gave them freehold ownership. President Nyerere of Tanzania summarised the matter: 'The extraordinary concept of land as a marketable commodity is quite foreign to us.' 'All human beings… were born to find land in existence. They can neither add to it nor reduce its extent. It is God's gift, given to all.'[52] Those whose feet have direct contact with the land may have an advantage. We who wear shoes, and, even more, we who move on tyres, we for whom earth is mostly hidden under tarmac or concrete, we need to recall the sense that the land is precious; the actual stuff of earth is a gift. Even just a few minutes of digging in our garden can bring us to our senses. Touch the ground; feel it even through your shoes. Recognise that it is not just another commodity, it is the basis of our living. Take your shoes off your feet, for it is holy ground (Exodus 3:5). I have seen a burning bush. In the middle of a fairly arid field in parched farmland in the area of my first appointment in South Africa, there was a little bush which I passed almost daily; at its roots there was a vent of methane gas, which was often ignited. The fact that there was a material explanation did not matter; the experience of seeing it was an experience of spirit, as it was for Moses. The bush could still do what the bush did for Moses: it aroused his curiosity. The simple fact that you have to ask 'Why' can lead you into a truth of spirit. The place is God's. You don't have to be Moses; you don't have to be in a special 'holy' place. Wherever you are standing is holy. The earth is the Creator's gift to you, like the air that you breathe. Be curious about it; ask it what it is. These are the questions of science, questions about matter. They are Moses' questions; and they can lead to spirit. The response to your 'Why' may be that you hear God's name. And your calling. You find yourself in the boundary-land of Creation.

Africa has received very little blessing from Christian authorities' obedience to the revealed will of God in the matter of land. As Archbishop Desmond Tutu has remarked: 'At first, they had the Bible and we had the land. Now, without anyone noticing, we have the Bible and they have the land.' I offer just one example out of many, which happens to be close to my own observation. On all official maps, the western boundary of Lesotho is called the Caledon River. The Basotho people have always called it the Mohokare. For hundreds of years, a large area of good agricultural land to the west of that river was held by Basotho for pasture and crops. In 1869, without any consultation with the Basotho, the British and the Boers made a treaty to incorporate that land into the Orange Free State, occupied and ruled by white settlers. They declared that the river should henceforth be the western boundary of the Basotho land. They celebrated its new status by changing its name to Caledon. Now the only fertile stretch of land left for the Basotho is the two miles wide strip east of the river, between the river and the mountains. And so Lesotho has become an economic dependency of South Africa, a source of cheap migrant labour.[53]

Legally-authorised segregation in land-use in South Africa goes back to long before the establishment of the apartheid regime. The 1913 Natives Land Act, passed under the British-based rule, allocated just 7 per cent of the arable land for the African people, who were 67 per cent of the population. The current President, Cyril Ramaphosa, has the Sabbath law on his side when he calls this 'the original sin'. But it is one thing to see the fault, and quite another to discover a just and practical means of putting it right, as the tragic example of Zimbabwe has shown.

New governments have come in many parts of Africa, replacing

European-dominated administrations that are skilled in drawing lines on maps. But nobody has yet succeeded in changing the boundaries which were convenient for the colonials. People tried to do something about this, in Biafra, and it led to one of the great tragedies of the twentieth century. It was not only the surface fertility of the land which attracted colonising powers. South Africa, like many other areas, became an area for conquest on account of what lies underneath: gold, diamonds, coal. But, there is plenty of evidence in our Scriptures to show that the authors knew about the use of minerals, but never any suggestion that there could be separation of agrarian rights from mineral rights, or a division between rights to the surface of land and separate rights for the exploitation of what lies below the surface. When the biggest cement manufacturer in the world wanted to develop a huge quarry in the Scottish Isle of Harris, it offered to help local people with a characteristic bargain; it promised to 'relieve unemployment provided the people surrendered their guardianship of the land.'[54] Mercifully, after popular protest, the proposal was eventually withdrawn.

Our faith tells us that the land comes to us from God, as a loan from God, a gift from our ancestors, on trust for the yet unborn. This way of justice lies deep in the heredity of our faith. But it doesn't look like that. An alien culture comes in which claims mastery over the land, and treats it in the same way as it treats other commodities. But it still remains true, that land is fundamentally different from anything else. We can make chairs and computers by our skill and hard work; we can work with the land to produce wheat and beetroot and apples; but we did not make the land. We can indeed almost destroy it, with violence and careless exploitation. But we cannot create it. It is absolutely limited.[55]

This is all central to the Sabbath provisions. The Bible Society recently published a series of essays on the theme of 'Mercy'.[56] Of the seven contributors, two chose to concentrate on a part of the Bible which, at first sight, might not be an obvious specimen of mercifulness, namely the book of Leviticus. But this was absolutely right. Leviticus 25 represents the fulfilment of the mercy of the Sabbath in its interruption of the inevitable processes of profit and loss, of success and failure, of domination and oppression. This is expressed particularly in the provisions concerning land-tenure. In South Africa, it was specifically to Leviticus 25 that I found myself being directed, as we tried to discern the ethical mandates that the scriptures might supply; it became clear that the notion of outright ownership of land in perpetuity was very far both from the African concept of land-tenure and from that of the Scriptures. But you will not find much about land-tenure in any standard Christian textbook on ethics.

The vision of the Mosaic Law is that every family has, in principle and in origin, an equal share in land-rights; but, over time, through hazards of good or ill fortune, of mistakes, accidents, bad luck, or stupidity, inequalities creep in. Some win, some lose. But not permanently. Every seven years, there is to be a Sabbatical Year, proclaimed on the Day of Atonement, in which debts are cancelled. This is another wisdom which the exiled Israelites owe to the influence of their oppressive masters in Babylon. The Babylonians realised that an economy of permanently unresolved indebtedness is bad politics. To maintain an army, to maintain a society of responsible citizens, there needs to be a core population that is not encumbered with personal debts. A system of restoration is required, a provision of a Clean Slate. So this was provided for in the laws of Hammurabi. It became the expected routine when a new king took office. 'Economists look at ancient Near-Eastern history and think, "You can't have Clean Slates, you can't have cancelled debts, because that will cause anarchy." The fact is that proclaiming a Clean Slate is the way to avoid anarchy, the way to restore self-sufficiency. So in Babylon, every ruler would from time to time proclaim a cancellation of debts, a new start, a Clean Slate.'[57] The mentors of the Hebrew people picked up this element of the Babylonian administration and built it into their own vision of an orderly community.

The need for some sort of provision concerning indebtedness is recognised in many civilisations; in western culture, we have necessary procedures for the administration of bankruptcy. But the Hebrews widened the scope of the models that they learned from Babylon. They made the Clean Slate idea a matter of theology as well as a means of forming an efficient society. It becomes a revelation of the mercy of the Creator. So it is to be a routine, a limitation on the exclusion of people from responsible citizenship. Every seven years, debts are to be cancelled, and slaves are to be released (Deuteronomy 15:1–18). This is to be done, not legalistically, not with an eye to getting away with the necessary minimum, but reflecting the Creator's generosity, the Lord's compassion on losers, reaching up, in Martin Luther King's fine phrase, 'to the majestic heights of the unenforceable'.[58]

Every seven Sabbatical Years, every 50 years, in every generation, there is to be a Jubilee Year; any inequalities in land-tenure are corrected, a new period of lease of the land commences. Land which has been accumulated and monopolised by a few is redistributed. Any trading which is done is trading in the use of the land for the period of the lease, or in the product of work on the land, not of the land on which the work has been performed. 'The land shall not be sold in perpetuity,' says God, 'for the land is mine and you are tenants' (Leviticus 25:23). Everybody has a stake in the land, is a sharer in the gift which God gives to the human race on loan. This is mercy. It is active intervention on behalf of those who, in one way or another, have been failures.

This is all very close to home. Some like to think of Britain as a property-owning democracy, where every young person ought to be aiming at getting onto the property-ladder. But for many families this is simply untrue. If that is the proper image of citizenship, many are non-citizens. The 'right to buy' did bring a lot of people into ownership, but local authorities have not been allowed to use the income from those sales to build new homes for rent. Local authorities' housing-stock for rental has got steadily smaller – virtually to zero in some small rural communities – so people who need homes to rent face endless disappointment. The place of local authorities in the housing of our people has been scaled down, and a traditional reservoir of expertise in this field has wasted away.

Others of us are landowners. We have freehold possession. We expect, for no good moral reason, that the value of our property will increase, without any action on our part except for waiting. The community around us may take action which happens to increase that value. The community, through its public authorities, builds roads, provides schools, organises the protection of police and emergency services, and the value of the land increases. Sometimes, a landowner can obstruct useful development simply by waiting until the value of the land is increased by the actions of other people. As a local Councillor, I have noticed how this sort of process is constantly affecting land-values, and, thereby reduces the ability of individuals to gain access to housing.

What responses are open to us, in terms of practical politics? The Community Infrastructure Levy provisions came into force in 2010. They do go some way in the direction of a tax on increase of value. The Levy is, in effect, a tax payable by developers to local councils on the income which they receive from the purchasers of new properties. So this provides occasional sources of revenue towards the facilities that councils provide, such as street-lighting. It can encourage councils to support development, and to be critical of residents' 'nimbyish' resistance to proposals for development – arguments which in practice occupy much of parish councils' agendas. But it does not apply to affordable housing development, and it does little to discourage developers' stratagems for evading their responsibility to include affordable housing in their plans. It applies only on new development and in effect simply increases the price of the property for the first purchaser. So it has no on-going effect on the culture of speculation in land values. But it is, arguably, a step in the right direction.

A better example happened just over one hundred years ago, when Johannesburg was rapidly expanding and an area of fairly poor land to the east of the city suddenly increased in value in the development of new suburbs. The Municipality imposed a tax, not on the developers but on the land-owners who were selling their stands to the developers. The Municipality used this revenue specifically to extend the public tramway passenger transport system into the new suburbs. This made the new properties more valuable, the benefit went to the developers and the new property-owners; it was a benefit that required the initiative of the political authority, which none of the other players could provide.

Nearly eighty years ago, Archbishop William Temple could make the apparently simple and obvious comment, 'There is no reason why we should pay certain citizens large sums of money for merely owning the land on which our cities are built.'[59] And before him, Winston Churchill identified the 'land monopolist' as one who 'contributes nothing to the process from which his own enrichment is derived'.[60] Things have not changed much in the meantime. In 2005, the Zacchaeus 2000 Trust produced an authoritative and detailed 'Memorandum to the Prime Minister on Unaffordable Housing', which proposed, among many other recommendations, the devising of a policy on Land Value Taxation.[61] This would give practical application to the Levitical principle that the value of the land should be the patrimony of the whole community. Private ownership or enclosure of land would be allowed on condition of payment of a fair fee for such privilege to the community as a whole. This was the vision of that once-influential, but now neglected, politician and visionary Henry George; he advocated not the nationalisation of land but the claiming of the rent-value of the land for the public exchequer.[62] To do this we would have to sort out one of the real practical problems in our British market-system; we would have to distinguish between the value of the land and the value of the development on the land. In some places, this is done; in Pennsylvania several municipalities have adopted a split-rate system, whereby tax is raised on the value of the land at one level and on the development on the land – i.e. the effect of human activity on the land – at another.[63] In Britain, at present, it is very difficult to figure out how the total value of a 'property' adds up. It is not the development on our land which has been causing massive rises in housing costs. The cost of bricks and timber has not been varying significantly beyond general inflation. What has been fluctuating out of control is the value of the land on which the development has been made, sometimes soaring (and some newspapers rejoice at this and tell their readers that it is wonderful news), and sometimes trapping householders in negative equity. The Levitical principle would provide greater stability.

We assume that ownership of land gives us the right, not only to develop the specific area that we own but also to control what happens to surrounding properties. Considerations like 'it will spoil our view' claim many hours of local councils' attention. This is not a new problem. It can claim a theological response. In the 1930s, Charles Jenkinson was appointed as priest of a very poor area of Leeds. He quickly decided that he could not continue to baptise infants unless he did something about the rats which were wrecking the life-chances of the youngest of his parishioners. While remaining a parish priest, he became leader of the Leeds Labour Party and Chair of the City Council Housing Department; he devised and supervised one of the biggest slum-clearance programmes in Europe. This was in face of powerful and well-funded opposition. He had to speak at many meetings to interpret the programme to the citizens and ratepayers of Leeds. At one such gathering, a gentleman stood up and said: 'I quite understand that you have to do something to improve the conditions for these poor people; but why are you sending them to live near me in Moortown?'. Jenkinson replied: 'I will answer your question with another question. Who the devil are you? And who the devil am I? And who the devil is anyone to say, "My fellow-man is not to live where I live"?' And he went on to give his theological reasoning: 'I, as a priest of the Catholic Church, am bound to admit to the family of God, with the same baptismal service, the child of a prince, or of a prostitute, or of a drunkard.' We don't know what the questioner made of this. But the houses of Jenkinson's new estates are still very much in business eighty years later.[64]

While I am writing this, the enquiry into the Grenfell Tower disaster is proceeding in its lengthy exploration. What caused that fire? The immediate answer is that its rapid spread was caused by the inflammable material used for the Tower's cladding. That was a cause, in the realm of matter; but finding a reason is more difficult than identifying a cause – this means a search in the realm of spirit. The more difficult question is: why was such cladding used? In whose interest was it applied? What motives steered that decision? Was it in the interest of the tenants, the relatively poor inhabitants of the Tower? Or was it in the interest of the vastly wealthy owners of neighbouring land, to improve the aesthetic value of their environment? Inevitably, a lot of anger is directed at the local authority; but a local authority will find it very difficult to resist the interests of the most privileged of their electorate.

A significant proportion of people in social housing are disabled, in one way or another. The Levitical code does not make special mention of such people; but its total intention is a just sharing of wealth across the community, for the fortunate and for the less fortunate. The requirements for affordable homes and for accessible homes belong together. But in present practice different local authorities differ a great deal from each other in their provision. There must be very few families which are not affected by disability in one form or another. But it counts strangely low on the agenda of the electorate, and therefore does not make the claim which it should make on the energies of policy-makers.[65]

In the Mosaic Law, there is special provision on behalf of citizens who do not have land-rights. There was one tribe of the people of Israel, the Levites, who had special duties which prevented them for owning land. They did not have the same land-rights as the rest of the community. They were to receive from the community a financial payment in lieu. That payment was not a stipend as reward for the Levites' service to the community; it was financial compensation for their loss of land-rights (Numbers 18:21ff.).

In this country, tenants do not get compensation for the fact that they are not property-holders; they are not part of the property-owning democracy. They are at a disadvantage in that they do not share in the rises in land-values created by the efforts of the community; they have nothing to bequeath to their inheritors. In Fred Harrison's view, they have been the victims, over many centuries, of the systematic cheating by the propertied classes, including royalty, in a system where land rent has been steadily diminished as a source of public revenue.[66] Over the centuries, the 'commons' – land which had been accessible for use by the whole community – were increasingly enclosed as private property. Peasants ceased to have access to land by right. Land became a marketable commodity, depending on money-wealth as means of possession. The only way for peasants to get land was by selling their labour, and by becoming rich enough to be able to purchase. 'But working to accumulate enough wealth to buy land, instead of assuming an inherent human birthright to the earth, is akin to a slave's saving enough money, by cleverness, skill and extra hard effort, to buy him or herself into freedom.'[67] Concerning slavery of that ancient kind, a small group of Christians in the nineteenth century was driven by a biblically-formed conscience to lead the way in proclaiming that slavery is incompatible with the mandates of God's rule; the same could be true in respect of access to land.

A Christian contribution to this issue could well consist of a serious evaluation of the assumptions concerning the 'property-owning democracy' in our society. Is this ideal really worth the problems that it raises and the injustices which it perpetuates? Our continental neighbours seem to be content with a general culture of rental of residential resources, even for the more privileged; and leasehold provision can, in principal, be equitable and effective. But this would go against the grain of our British assumptions, and would not be practical politics in our present political system. Only a non-political organisation would have the freedom to ask such questions.

But all is not lost. Even in an island country, where land is precious, we still preserve land which is held 'in common' – in the corporate assets of parks and wetlands and public gardens. Both in public opinion and in council policy, we need to be vigilant in protecting such spaces, for they are Sabbath-mercies. The church, in its various forms and traditions, has particular responsibility for Sabbath-spaces of this kind, in its churchyards and grave-spaces (see note 68, below). The church building itself, in its space on the land, stands for Sabbath. It is an interruption to the rows of houses or the institutions of industry and commerce. Sometimes, we try to identify with the environment by putting up a church building which looks like a factory or a council headquarters; fine – a worthy intention. But more often, it looks embarrassingly different; and that can be an advantage, because its mandate is indeed to be different, to be a structure of defiance. It gives space for us to look around ourselves and to see things from a viewpoint that is different from the aims of the financial economy and the appeal of competitive acquisition. It is a place where all are equal, equal in our baptism, equal in our sharing in the Body and the Blood of the Lord of the Sabbath. It is where we bring our skills, our professional identities, our relationships, but to offer them, not to be defined by them. It is a place where, in the processes of confession and absolution, we can be totally honest with ourselves, where we can be delivered from our anxieties about our moral success and failure. It is, in a word, a place of worship, a place dedicated to the affirmation that 'the earth is the Lord's'. It is a place from which we can see with Sabbath-trained eyes and recognise that the houses next door and the institutions of work and the fields of production are also parts of the earth that is the Lord's.

There are other places around which look different to the

contemporary norm. Sometimes, next door to the church, there is another old building, built with the same technology and materials as the church. But it is redundant, obsolete, because its purpose was not the worship of God but the securing of a structure of domination. The church is serving the purpose for which it was originally built, and is maintained by the generous commitment of its amateur contemporary members. The castle next door is an interesting relic, maintained professionally by some distant conservation authority. Its purpose has fallen away. Materially it is much the same as the church; spiritually it is part of the system which the church is in business to defy. The spiritual difference can be very obvious; there is a loving enthusiasm in the one which is just not there in the other. The fact that the castle is now dead, a useless museum piece, like chastity belts, is a mercy. The fact that the church is alive and used for its original purpose, is also a mercy, part of the evidence of God's claim on the earth.[68]

And we can look out at other forms of 'commons', such as airwaves, seeds, aspects of the DNA code, water and air, which in principle are the common inheritance of humankind. We can see that these also are of the earth that is the Lord's. If they become 'enclosed' as commercial commodities within the market, if they are taken from common access into the property of profit-seeking sections of society, they also are being stolen from the Lord.

Our vigilance in these matters can be derived directly from our obedience to the mandates of the Seventh Day of Creation. Our doctrine of Creation tells of a God who intervenes in the fatalisms of the market, who re-creates according to God's intention of justice and mercy. A doctrine of Creation which does not have this intentional bias is not the doctrine which the Scriptures offer to us.

8.

The Seventh Day

Connecting to Learning

The first two mercies offered by the Seventh Day can be entitled Labour and Land. The third mercy is Learning.

The Sabbatical year provides a period of in-service training for the whole community (Deuteronomy 31:9–13). In recent years, the word 'Sabbatical' has been claimed on behalf of the academically successful. It is a provision which gives the intellectual high-fliers a break from their routine duties, so that they can do something different and fly a bit higher. We need not grudge them such a privilege: indeed, I did once have a plan for a Sabbatical myself, but it was torpedoed by the South African government. However, in the Mosaic Law, the purpose of the Sabbatical is just the opposite, and we should not allow the academically privileged to steal the nomenclature. In Deuteronomy, the whole community of the land is given time off from their routines, to be brought up to date in their knowledge of the law. By 'law' is meant not only the rules of legal and civil and religious obedience but also the whole range of knowledge, with no boundary between sacred and secular – history, agriculture, marital and sexual behaviour, sanitation, animal welfare, dietetics, theology, land-tenure, census studies, environmental responsibility, the creation and distribution of wealth, employment and working conditions, the rights of aliens, and all the other areas of knowledge which are dealt with in the Hebrew books of the law. In many places in the Hebrew law, there is the assumption that the law is organised by males and that it is to be implemented by males. But at this point it is clear that it is addressed to the whole community. Men, women, and children are to hear the law and are to be treated as responsible citizens in response to the law.

Just as the Sabbath regulations concerning Labour were designed to prevent the emergence of an élite of employers served by a voiceless proletariat of slaves, and just as the regulations concerning Land were devised to prevent a small clique of landowners from dominating a population of landless paupers, so this element of the Sabbatical Year was designed to prevent society from being divided into an oligarchy of experts presiding over an ignorant mob of peasants. For a trusting community to develop, knowledge needs to be shared. Knowledge is for all, and is not to be restricted to those who can pay for it. This is the mandate for Adult Education, the WEA, the Open University, the whole Further Education sector. The Sabbatical Year is part of our Creator's intention. Our Creator is the God of the Second Chance, the one who makes space for those who have missed out on previous opportunities, who does not wish us to be limited by the accidents of our starting-point. This is God's mercy. We should not overlook the contribution to the sharing of knowledge which can be enabled by modern technology: peasants working far from the big city can discover, on their mobile phones, what are the current values in the city market, and so can be better able to claim a proper price for their produce.

Pope Francis has noted how the discussions about such matters as the environment and international economic problems are mostly conducted by people who 'live and reason from the comfortable position of a high level of development and a quality of life beyond the reach of the majority of the world's population'.[69] They tend to treat problems of the poor as merely collateral damage. On matters of ecology, it is essential that we hear the cry of the poor themselves. The Sabbatical Year is designed to enable the voiceless to join in the conversation. The church which is inspired by the mandates of Creation will enable that voice to be heard; for instance, Archbishop Winston Halapua of Polynesia points out how rising sea levels, which may cause some inconvenience to the powerful in the world, are threatening total loss to poor people in the islands of the Pacific. 'While they are amongst the lowest carbon emitters in the world, they will be the first to suffer from climate change.'[70] The Astronomer Royal underlines this claim, with the warning that 'climate change will hit hardest those who have contributed least to its cause. Heat stress will hurt most those without air-conditioning; crop failure will most affect those who already struggle to afford food; extreme weather events will most endanger those whose homes are fragile.'[71] But, like all poor people, these voices are not to be heard as only victims and complainers. As Archbishop Halapua shows, the island communities of Oceania are able to offer us their *theomoana,* their God-talk based on their experience of the ocean. They create an enriching theology which is not sourced from the established academies of the west, which, even in our 'island nation', are not noticeably dominated by sea-farers. This theology can expand our understanding of our Creator, as one who is beyond the limitations of boundaries and definitions, who enables communication and sharing between communities.[72] That can offer healing and expansion for our land-based images and mandates of the Sabbath, of the Church, and of God. The loss of such a voice would be an impoverishment of the whole Christian family.

The 'Law', as we have noted, covers a wide range of subject matter; but, among all the other subjects, it does include the law, in the narrower sense. Where people are ill-informed about their rights under the law, they can be at as much of a disadvantage under good law as they can be under bad. Under the apartheid regime in South Africa, it was only too easy for the police to make up the law as they went along, depending on poor people's ignorance of their rights. Some of us felt that one of the duties of the church was to help people to understand where the law could be of advantage to them, particularly concerning the rights of defendants, of accused persons, and of witnesses. Jesus gave a classic example of how his followers should affirm the rule of law, when he responded to a policeman who was treating him as guilty before he had been found guilty: 'If I spoke amiss, state it in evidence; if not, why do you strike me?' (John 18:17, a text which we often found useful in protests in South Africa). Where knowledge of the law is shared, everyone has a stake in the law; everyone can be on the guard against abuses such as discrimination against people who are poor or disabled or homeless. As a Councillor, on behalf of the citizens of our area, I see it as part of our duty to be vigilant concerning access to the law. At present, in Britain, we see gradual reduction in the availability of Legal Aid. Further, in a semi-rural area such as North Shropshire, where I live, we see the closure, one by one, of the Magistrates' Courts which have served our citizens. That is one of the penalties of being in a borderland – we are easily forgotten by those who make decisions in large buildings. The institutions of justice move further and further away from us. Justice which is made inaccessible becomes justice denied. The law of Sabbath would encourage citizens to be watchful; the more we understand the law the more we will feel that it is worth protecting.

Nearly 100 years ago, T. S. Eliot was asking: 'Where is the

wisdom we have lost in knowledge? Where is the knowledge we have lost in information?'[73] The Learning that is provided in the regulations about Sabbath is offered as an aspect of the Law of the Creator; it is about obedience to the purposes of the Creator. Therefore, it is mainly about matters of value rather than of information for information's sake. That does not fit very comfortably into our present sense of priorities in education. At one stage of my life, I was engaged as a kind of 'guest lecturer' in a College of Education, and therefore was invited to supply questions to be included in the subsequent exams. I tried to provide questions on the lines of, 'in what ways do you think that this or that piece of learning is going to be useful in handling this or that type of problem?'. I was told that this sort of question was unconventional; it was allowable, but only as one of several more factual alternatives. The last couple of hundred years have seen huge increases in the volume of available information. This is obvious in the natural sciences, and it is rightly given immense value. It can affect other disciplines. As people who were supposed to be teaching theology, I remember well the sharp comment of my beloved colleague Lesslie Newbigin, who compared the contemporary style of teaching in our profession with that of the teachers of his nephew, who was studying architecture; in that discipline, the essential criterion for their teaching was, 'How far is this going to help the student to become a good practitioner?' The teaching prescribed in Deuteronomy was essentially purposive, designed to help the people to function as a liberated community. Similarly with the teaching of Jesus; he gave his students sandwich-courses, with his theoretical instruction about the Kingdom of God alternating with practice out in the field. As I mentioned earlier, I felt occasional disappointment in my university studies. I was used to the purposiveness of my training in the RAF ('If you can't get your oleo-leg pressures more accurate than that, some poor bugger is going to get killed!'[74]). Studying to be able to put BA after one's name seemed to be settling for a rather lower target. The effect of biblical teaching is not to be measured in terms of individual qualifications but in terms of the values of a Sabbath-inspired community. And, in fairness to the University, when I rejected sensible advice and completely changed direction by switching to Divinity for my third year, I found teachers like John Burnaby and Michael Ramsey, who taught their subject as if it really *mattered* to themselves and to the world's truth. They have been inspiration to me ever since.

We have seen that, in the programmes concerning Labour and Land, the Sabbath Law requires care and hard work. But it still remains Sabbath, the rule of rest, of space, and blessing. The same is true in the programme concerning Learning. When I pause to think carefully about whether to write a sentence, the screen goes blank. That friendly message appears. The mandate in Deuteronomy for the sharing of knowledge is part of the Sabbath mandate. It is part of the interruption of our activism, our habitual information-gathering exercise. It depends on other things giving way and providing space. It is part of the Sabbath liberation.

The Learning that is provided in the Sabbath regulations is the gift of the Creator, the bringer of light. But, in the Hebrew Scriptures and in the New Testament, there are many warnings against untruth, against teachers who conspire against the light by claiming to be light. There are devices of the powerful, both ancient and modern, where light is used as a cruel and penetrating intrusion – the simple torture of being locked in a cell where the light is always on and you have no access to the switch; the pressure to betray one's colleagues, where perjury may be the lesser sin; the light which searches out every deviation from the norms specified by those who set the rules; the flash mounted next to the lens, which overrules the modelling of cheekbones and the glistening of stubble; the streetlights which abolish midnight.[75] The London-Welsh poet and painter David Jones puts a beautiful prayer into the heart of a pre-Christian Celtic peasant, struggling against the cultural power-systems of a colonial administration which seeks to 'proscribe the diverse uses and impose the rootless uniformities'; he prays to a local spirit of wood or well, to the 'queen of otherness, the mistress of asymmetry':

'In the bland megalopolitan light

Where no shadow is by day or by night

Be our shadow.'[76]

Yes, a prayer to a traditional spirit of the Celtic world; but it would be equally appropriate to call on the Mother of Bethlehem in such terms.

In a totally different context, Bonhoeffer warned against 'the fanatical devotee of truth... who wounds shame, desecrates mystery, betrays the community in which he lives, and laughs arrogantly at the devastation which he has wrought. He feels like a god above those feeble creatures and does not know that he is serving Satan. God's truth judges created things out of love, and Satan's truth judges them out of envy and hatred. God's truth has become flesh in the world, but Satan's truth is the death of all reality.'[77]

In short, an accurate statement may be untrue. Its use falsifies its validity. Its light is being used against the purposes of the Creator.

St Patrick, according to the version of his Breastplate made accessible to us by the Irish poet Mrs Cecil Frances Alexander, prayed that Christ would protect us 'against the knowledge that defiles.'[78]

The knowledge that we can get by modern communications systems is not necessarily incorrect. Abusive betrayal of children, the advertising that encourages persistent dissatisfaction, the selection of injurious details about people whom we don't like, the quotation of incautious remarks out of context – these may all be correct information. But they defile. They claim to enlighten, but in effect they deepen the darkness. They are 'Satan's spells and wiles'. Patrick was praying long before the invention of the internet. Jones did not know how the neon tube and the LED would become ubiquitous. Bonhoeffer did not need the corruptions of social media to show how evil can impressively parade as the light. But the vitality of their perceptions has become even more apparent with the arrival of our present century.

The Sabbath programme is to enable knowledge to be shared for the common good, not to be a commodity for the advantage of a privileged few. That advantage can be simply a demonstration of rival cleverness, of making simple people feel stupid. Elias Chacour, the Palestinian Archbishop of Galilee, accused Christian groups of this kind of misuse of the light. 'Christians have wanted to be distinguished and famous instead of using the light in such a way that people can see past us and discover their saviour. I can hear the Third World, the non-Christian world, saying, Yes, you Christians, you may be the light, but please dim your headlights, you are blinding us with your brightness, we cannot see where we are going because of your blinding light… Allow us to see Jesus. Dim your lights.'[79]

The Sabbath provisions concerning Learning show that the authorities of religion and culture have a duty to ensure that information is shared with the whole community. This is to be done under the authority of the Creator, not to serve the partisan interests of a section of the community, or to enable clever people to score points. The 'common people' have to be trusted. The disciple-community has a corporate responsibility for discernment. There are two criteria: first, is the information compatible with the witness that light has come in Jesus Christ? And second, does the information serve to strengthen the fellowship of love and mutual service (1 John 4)? We have the severe warning, that if we accept as light that which is truly darkness, that darkness is total (Matthew 6:23).

Those who set up in business to be conveyers of truth have a very particular responsibility. The more learned we are the more damage we can do. Hendrik Verwoerd, the South African Prime Minister who was recognised as the primary theorist of the ideology of apartheid, was a brilliant student who was appointed to a Chair of applied psychology at the age of 26. In daily practice, apartheid was experienced, by black people and other opponents of the system, as almost mindless thuggery, carried out by officials of the state who made up the rules as they went along. But its leaders were not barnstormers of mesmerising oratory. They were coldly intellectual planners – their second Prime Minister, J. C. Strijdom, was so boringly predictable in his speeches that journalists used to write reports of what he had said before the event took place and to send them in without actually attending, and he would then compliment them on their accuracy. Apartheid had a thoroughly coherent prospectus, in political, philosophical, and theological terms. But it was a demonic ideology; when it failed, major churches found that they had to repent of the support which they had given.

Forty years ago, after the Watergate scandal, the American Association of University Professors issued a statement acknowledging, with grief, that all the persons involved were graduates of American institutions of Higher Education, and regretting that 'we had failed to help them to overcome their character defects while they were in our tutelage'. Do we hear similar acknowledgements concerning the various disorders in our present society, which have been brought about by clever misleaders?

The Sabbath provisions make it clear that the sharing of truth is not simply a human industry; it is a responsibility under the direct authority of the Creator. Those who find themselves called to be the fulfillers of these provisions are answerable not merely to public opinion or to professional standards, but to the Source of Truth and Law.

The provisions of the Sabbath, of the Sabbatical Year, and of the Jubilee, are the gift of the Creator, who makes community out of a rabble of liberated slaves. Like the Ten Commandments, they are designed to maintain the community in continuous creation. But God's will is not automatically fulfilled. Sabbathlessness is attractive. The powerful will want to have a Sabbathless society, in which slaves are not released, production continues 24/7, the land has no rest, exploitation is not curbed, people with disabilities are treated as valueless, an ignorant underclass is maintained, the distinction between owners and non-owners is affirmed, and nothing will interrupt, nothing will interfere with the power of some to command the menial service of others (Amos 8:4–6). In a word, Babylon stays in business. Babylon is here, in the various kinds of apartheid which divide our world, in the unresting power-systems against which we feel that we can never win. But there is still an alternative message. The Sabbath provisions are God's mercy; it's true that there's wideness in God's mercy, but it is equally true that there's a huge defiance in God's mercy. It is a mercy that stands against much in our culture. 'Almost everything about the origins of Christianity is abhorrent to the vested interests of today.'[80]

9.

The Sabbath

Fantasy or Reality?

We have given this book the title, 'Seven Days to Freedom'. This adequately summarises its main theme. But, unless we allow it to raise one or two sharp questions, it can be nothing better than an optimistic hoorah-slogan.

Freedom. Freedom for whom? During the past couple of centuries, there have been large and God-fearing nations which have fought sacrificial wars to affirm their right to keep slaves. In South Africa and among the descendants of the Confederacy in the southern USA, diligent citizens remember and celebrate those conflicts; they have cherished the idea of freedom which they have sought to deny to others. They treasure these memories with that special valuation of history which inspires peoples who, like the Welsh and Scots and Irish, know what it is like to have been defeated on their own territory. The English are unusual in that, as a nation, they have not had such an experience for the past thousand years.

The Creation-stories of the Hebrew Bible celebrate the God who is on the side of those to whom freedom has been denied, the slave, the outsider, the badly-placed. The freedom to exploit other people, the freedom to grasp the share of resources which properly belong to others, this is not the freedom offered by our Creator; and we need to be self-critical about the ways in which we celebrate or claim our freedom. Martin Luther saw his movement as a blessing of deliverance from the oppression of Rome; but he observed that some 'reformed' Christians thought that liberation from old law meant that the traditional duty of charitable giving no longer applied, and that they were free to sell their goods at the highest price that they could get. Luther saw this not as freedom but as a new bondage to Satan, and that these people were now 'in worse case than they were when they were under the bondage of the Pope'.[81] The liberating Law of Leviticus 25 will be a restriction on some; in God's community there will be no room for the kind of exploitation which the privileged Babylonians inflicted on their menial fellow-humans. The quality of a community's freedom can be measured from the degree of equality among the members – see 2 Corinthians 8:13; indeed, the whole message of 2 Corinthians 8 and 9 provides a very practical programme for the spirit of genuine freedom. So the way of God's freedom, in matters of Land, Labour, and Learning, will require careful planning and scrutiny. It will require a stable administration and an incorrupt bureaucracy.

The Sabbath Law will require strong central government. In our present culture, much of the wealth created by the work of the community can be shifted around, transferred to agencies outside the control of central government and inaccessible to taxation. But the Levitical order was a response to crisis, the continued crisis of the possibility that God might abandon the people and consign them to a renewal of transportation and exile. In our culture we know very well that, in a crisis, government responds by strengthening its power and control, and the community, perhaps reluctantly, accepts this. The crisis of war brings food rationing, and the public accepts. The crisis of road deaths leads to a sheaf of regulations about speed, drink-driving and seat-belts. The present crisis of terrorism brings a response of increased precautions on streets and at air-terminals. A financial crisis could well lead to a government-dominated central bank taking more control; it could apply more taxation on capital transfers which remove wealth into unaccountable off-shore hideaways. Thirty years ago, George MacLeod, the Founder of the Iona Community, was drawing attention to the dangers of the functioning of the international money-market, the operatives whom he called 'the money-boys'. More recently, Archbishop Welby has highlighted the same problems. The economist Ann Pettifor investigates this with practical precision. Born and nurtured in the South African goldfields, she has become an authority on debt-systems as they affect both poor and rich countries; she was largely responsible for the effectiveness of the Jubilee 2000 campaign. In a way which aligns well with the intention of this book, she especially develops connections, connections between the financial crisis and the even greater crisis of climate change. We have already noted ways in which this will be affecting some of the poorest areas of the world. As time quickly passes, we see the signs becoming steadily stronger. Unprecedented melting of ice is reshaping the functioning of our polar regions. Unprecedented fires devastate New South Wales and California. Unprecedented rainfall causes flooding to river-systems in Yorkshire and in the Severn-Wye-Monnow catchment area. Unprecedented crowds gather in protest in big cities, to demand action by governments world-wide. In an unprecedented debate in 2020, the Church of England General Synod rejected a motion requiring the church to achieve net-zero carbon emissions by 2045, substituting the date 2030. Almost any programme to reduce our national carbon footprint is bound to be costly to some. It will look like a reduction of freedom. It will require legal and political interference. There will have to be an end to the absurd situation where fuel costs for land transport incur tax but aviation fuel costs do not. The car which I am content to drive now will probably be illegal in twenty years' time, and there will be no provision for old bangers. Pettifor foresees that in order to develop an appropriate programme of economic activity, 'the Finance Minister will need to consider two kinds of capacity, the potential capacity of the economy and the available capacity of the ecosystem.'[82] As result, the citizen may have to face two forms of rationing: a rationing of food and a rationing of carbon use. In ordinary circumstances, this would seem to be an unacceptable increase in Government's powers to interfere in the economy. But the coronavirus crisis has taken on the character of a crisis of war, and a Conservative government has been behaving in a way that would have been unthinkable at the beginning of 2020. If Government can recognise that the environmental crisis is just as demanding, we may see Pettifor's remedy taking shape. Perhaps, the pressing need for international co-operation in combating the virus may lead governments to co-operate more in facing the environmental crisis. The virus is already unleashing remarkable co-operation between citizens in care for each other; could this become true for nations too? The original Sabbath mandates must have caused considerable resentment, and denial of the necessity. A church which takes the Sabbath seriously could help the public to be ready for such possibilities, in the belief that the principle of sharing will make sense for a community that believes in God as Creator. Freedom has to be freedom first for those who at present are denied freedom.

A second sharp question follows: did the Sabbath system

work? In the last three chapters, we seem to have come a long way from the simple mandate of the Seventh Day that it is for our resting. A large edifice of rules and procedures has been prescribed, requiring a stable and reasonably independent national structure, with a competent and incorruptible bureaucracy to operate it. Were the Hebrews ever able to develop such a counter-culture against the norms of the surrounding nations? Is Leviticus 25 anything more than a utopian fantasy? The indications are very mixed. We cannot know for sure how far the detailed regulations were put into effect. What is clear is that the Sabbath institution remains central to Jewish identity; Leviticus 25 and the other Sabbath ideals remain as part of the Hebrew Scriptures, with their claim upon corporate conscience of the children of Abraham. For Josephus, in the New Testament era, they were current and significant.[83] When Greek invaders conquered Jews, they were surprised by the extent to which the land was worked by small-holders; but the invaders, with a different theology, regarded conquered land as their property, so they disenfranchised the small-holders.[84] The warnings of Isaiah 5:8 and Deuteronomy 15:1–11 and 26:17 do not appear to have influenced the approach of modern Israel in its policies towards settlement on land occupied by Palestinians.[85] Still less have they found their way into the mindset of European nations with Christian inheritance. The persistent mandate of the Hebrew Scriptures is to remember the 'stranger', the alien. This remains an indelible element in the theology of mercy, for Jew and Christian alike; but it has very mixed implementation in our practical obedience.

The first Christians found that the effect of the blessing of the Holy Spirit was to lead them into a Jubilee-style of sharing in goods and a continuing experience of puncturing boundaries. But even in those early days, the Christian faithful had to be reminded of their ethical roots. In that most Jewish of the New Testament letters, James has to warn against the economic apartheids being displayed within the common life of the congregation (James 5:1–6). And, not very much later, the Christian movement became infected by the Roman land-laws of property, based on conquest and plunder and enclosure. Their leaders had to protest along Sabbath-law lines against Babylonian life-styles creeping in: 'It was in common and for all that the earth was created. Why then, O rich, do you take to yourselves the monopoly of owning land? It is not with your wealth that you give to the poor, but with a fraction of their own that you give back, for you are usurping to yourself something meant for the common good of all.'[86] At about the same time, Pelagius, in spite of being labelled a heretic, was offering many observations of succinct truth, such as, 'Why would God want people to be unequal in the lesser things, when he has made them equal in the greater?'[87]

One underlying question must receive its answer from the examples of Sabbath that we have seen. Sabbath is 'Holy'. It is different to other days. What is its effect on the other days? Does it distinguish itself from them, or does it represent them? It is clear from mandates such as care for the stranger and widow that such a mandate cannot be confined to one day a week. In the Sabbath, we see that one day is holy, to represent the holiness of all days. One place is holy, to represent the holiness of all places. Some people are holy, to represent the holiness of all people. One baby is born in Bethlehem, and represents the God-like-ness of every baby. One man dies on a cross, representing the presence of the divine in every person who is treated as rubbish. Some bread is identified as the divine body, representing the holiness of all bread. And so on. The Sabbath is the clear example of God's way of claiming some in order to claim all. That is the principle of consecration, whether we are thinking of time or of place or of people or of things. So all time is holy; and the whole earth is the Lord's.

The Sabbath mandates maintain their continuing validity, beyond the boundaries which both secular and sacred might wish to maintain. So we look beyond boundaries, in a wide borderland. If ethical authorities do not intervene on behalf of the less powerful, decisions will be made to the advantage of the most powerful. Those who can pay for it will get. Forty years ago, the government of the United Kingdom had at its disposal the skills and the finance to authorise the construction of a machine that could convey a small number of people very expensively across the world at a speed higher than the speed of sound. It succeeded. It also had the skills and the finance to make permanent provision for the housing of the poorest communities of the nation. It did not succeed – and still has not done so. This was not a matter of science or technology; it was entirely a matter of motivation. And motivation is a spiritual matter. It is a matter of public ethics, of who decides what and how. Concorde was built, and it was an economic mistake; it did not sufficiently benefit those who held the power. So it was scrapped. The housing has still not been built. The claims of the common good have not had their motivating effect. And that is a spiritual matter. Who has charge of the nation's spirit, and on whose behalf? That is the question posed by the Sabbath vision. From where do we derive our ethical priorities? Both biblical history and modern history tell us that if technical and scientific and financial systems are not directed by an ethic of justice and compassion they will be co-opted to serve the interests of those who can pay; they won't be neutral for long. The message of the Seventh Day is that our total picture and understanding of Creation are to be shaped by its moral purpose. We can know what we do know about the processes of Creation by way of the discoveries of science; the wisdom of the spirit is not in business to compensate for what science has not yet discovered, but to give us resources for the just handling of what has already been discovered. The message of the Seventh Day is firmly there in our inheritance, but it is often a forgotten element of our unfinished agenda.

We have noted how God is recognised in the darkness, the darkness of which God is master, where he has set the boundaries. But the Scripture is clearly a structure of divine enlightenment, and especially so in the arrival in the world of the Christ, the light of the world. The light shines in the darkness, and the darkness has not mastered it (John 1:3). God is light, and in God there is no darkness (l John 1:5). But this enlightenment is not primarily a mental or aesthetic achievement. It is not just another pathway for the elevation of those who have the opportunity to become intellectually distinguished. It is not to be measured by the accumulation of information. As we have seen, the writer who is most emphatic about the Gospel of Light is St John. He makes it clear that the test and purpose of the Christ-light is the same as that of the Sabbath-light; it is to be recognised not in intellectual achievement but in the formation of community, in the fellowship of love, in the practical sharing of wealth (1 John 2:9–11, 3:17). It is all part of the divine purpose of mercy, of driving lovelessness from the Creation.

If this is the programme that we are to serve, are we then to bombard our local councillors with quotations from the Bible, to shower lots of free copies of extracts from the Book of Leviticus upon them? Well, it will do no harm for the general public to be told that provisions of this kind are indeed part of our historic culture, and that there are standards of public order which can be used as tests against our current routines and practices. But fundamentally, in the Scriptures, this is all part of the Holiness Code, and it was the particular duty of the priests to treasure it, to communicate it, and to apply it. In these days, we have specialists in law and administration, who are entrusted with responsibility for the ordering of society; and they can be justifiably irritated when the clergy appear to sound off about the economy in grand and abstract terms. I have to acknowledge that I have come to recognise many of the nuts and bolts of housing and land-tenure only since I retired from being a professional cleric; and Leviticus is, as we have seen, largely concerned with nuts and bolts. As Professor John Rogerson has said, in his Introduction to our volume about Leviticus in the 'Practice Interpretation' series, there is in it more practical instruction on how to do things than in any other book of the Bible.[88] It shows that the nuts and bolts of organising and administration are essential in society, that God is as much concerned about them as he is about the grand ideals. In our church life, we pray for and support our local councils; we are vigilant for the well-being of people who may be affected by failures in practical justice; and we try to encourage our local citizens to recognise that to 'love your neighbour' may mean asking awkward questions about affordable housing.

So the question can be put to our confirmation candidates, to our ordinands, to our congregations: In your learning about Christian faith, what are the issues that matter, in our obedience to God? The Church is in business to represent the mandates and character of our Creator. We go back to the basic truth that we are made in the image of God. This Social Holiness is a vital part of God's own self-disclosure. As our Creator's life-style is a life-style of Sabbath, so this is how God's human creation is intended to be.

And that is wonderful. It is admirable. It is something that is worth worshipping. That is an essential feature of the Law of the Lord. We have the law by the liberating grace of God, who has delivered us from slavery. We obey, not as part of a troublesome bargain, to earn the boss's favour, but to honour the blessing we have already received. We celebrate the truth about ourselves, the welcome we have received into God's plan. So the law is something that can arouse not only a sense of duty, not only a call to obedience, but delight. When the psalmists sing, 'Happy are those who delight in the law of the Lord' (Psalm 1) or 'I delight in the way of your decrees as much as in all riches' (Psalm 119), they are referring not just to the sublime generalities of the Ten Commandments but also to the day-to-day contents of the Law, with its details concerning debt and land-tenure and education-for-life. The Law is a way not only to justice but to happiness. How many of us in our culture are delighted by our laws? Surely we should include them in our thanksgivings. As Martin Luther King used to say: 'The law can't make you love me but it can restrain you from lynching me, and that's a good thing too.'[89] Where we are thankful – and there is indeed a great deal to be thankful for in the rule of law as we experience it day by day – we also value; and where we value, we are the more inspired to work for correction and improvement. I am no lawyer. Indeed, I have been on the wrong side of the law more than I care to remember. But I recognise that, to be effective, law has to be based on Truth – the way things actually are. And it has to be based on Wisdom – a realistic assessment of what is practicable, what is desirable, what truly makes for happiness. Julian of Norwich tells us how this can bring us to unexpected blessing: 'Truth sees God: wisdom gazes on God. And these two produce a third, a holy, wondering delight in God, which is love.'[90] If that is where a reflection on the Law can take us, bless the Creator for the Law!

Some law is expressed in imperatives: do this, don't do that. But many elements of the law are expressed in the future indicative: you shall do this, you shall not do that. This is true even of some of the Ten Commandments. The imperative is the power-word from the authority; we act as we are instructed, as robots do. 'You shall' tells us what our responsibility is; the effectiveness of the instruction is up to us. It enables. It declares our potential. Here is another way in which we are borderers, living in two ways of being. Nine of the Ten Commandments are, in principle, enforceable. They can be cited in testimony before a magistrate; guilt and innocence can be measured. But at the Tenth Commandment we enter the realm of the unenforceable. What magistrate can assess a degree of covetousness? Magistrate's law can tell us where we have come from; it is about behaviours that can be measured. Sabbath law is about where we may go. It tells us that, in the community of the liberated, 'you shall not covet'. That is the nature of the Sabbath; it declares not what is but what can be. This is the kind of world-view which inspired Nelson Mandela, and made him an inspiration to so many. A politician of his character can operate only in the strength of a potential, a vision of what could be. It can be realised; or, it can be hindered by corruption – as has been tragically true in that particular instance.[91]

So, there is a lot of activity and obedience involved in the provisions of Sabbath. But all the regulations are designed to enable a community of freedom. Sabbath is still the Seventh Day, the day of God's rest, the space of our Abiding in God. Sabbath is neither punishment nor reward; it is true being. Sabbath is gift, the gift of the liberating God. It is the institution of peace, not just a peace of heart but peace which is truly peace, a political peace. God's shalom is never just internal; it is essentially a peace that is *between*. The peace of Sabbath is freedom, but not freedom to exploit. It is not freedom at the expense of someone else's restriction It is not a freedom in which we are defined by our status as consumer. It is not a freedom to choose between different ways of dominating. It is not even a freedom of having made the most satisfying choice. It is the freedom of having been chosen, the freedom of being loved. It is gift.

Because we are chosen, we can freely choose; and that can have real practical effects. The year 1955 saw the tenth anniversary of the dropping of nuclear bombs on Hiroshima and Nagasaki. A high-powered international conference in Geneva took place on 'The Peaceful Uses of Atomic Energy', with specialist consultants and political leaders from all over the world. I happened to be near Geneva at that time with a group of our parishioners from Yorkshire, and it was a wonderful privilege to attend an ecumenical act of worship for the conference in the city's Cathedral. The preacher was the veteran ecumenical statesman, close friend of Dietrich Bonhoeffer, and Bishop of Chichester, George Bell. He took as his text Deuteronomy 30:19 – 'See,' God says to his chosen people, 'I have set before your life and death, good and evil. Choose life, so that you and your children may live…' That choice remains before us to this day. It is the choice for which Deuteronomy's message of Sabbath gives us the freedom, the knowledge, and the space to make, both responsibility and blessing.

10.

The Creator

To Believe and to Worship

This book is about making connections. Its intention is to suggest an integrated programme for making our belief in our Creator real and effective.

So: two parables.

A favourite sketch of Morecambe and Wise. A great symphony orchestra, conducted by André Previn, with solo pianoforte Eric Morecambe; the opening of the Grieg Piano Concerto in A minor, with the prominent role of the solo piano; splendid sound from orchestra, total confusion from soloist. 'Stop,' shouts conductor, and to the soloist: 'You are getting all the notes wrong.' 'No,' replies Morecambe, 'I am playing the right notes, but not necessarily in the right order.'

The following is a true story, which happens to be about my trade, but the same value would apply equally in the work of a cook or a carpenter or a chiropodist or a chemist. When I started as Rector of a group of village churches in Zululand, a young Zulu priest, Fr Msane, was serving as curate. He had been supplied with a motorbike for getting around the area – a 250cc BSA, quite sensible but on the light side for our terrain. He told me that it was losing power, so I checked it and found that it did indeed need an overhaul. There was no place nearby that could do such work, so I removed the engine unit from the frame and took it to a specialist in Durban, 120 miles away. When we got it back and reassembled it, we could not start it. I checked the ignition, all okay, and the fuel supply, all okay. So I took the cover off the valve-gear, and found the valves had been connected wrong – the push-rod for the exhaust valve had been connected to the inlet valve, and the push-rod for inlet valve had been connected to the exhaust valve. Connections were present, but out of order. I changed them round, and the engine started at first kick.

That's what this book is about. We are trying to follow the example set in the Scriptures, of connecting our faith with the nuts and bolts of our earthly life. Connections are there to be found, according to the purposes of the designer; our job is to get them in order.

I believe in God the Father Almighty, Maker of heaven and earth. If you can believe that, most of the rest of the creed is relatively simple. A lot is stacked against us. But that is, for me, not primarily because of problems with the science. I have great respect for the practitioners of the science-and-faith quest, and I have discussed some of these matters with people who know much more than I do about how the world works. But we note again Pope Francis's comment, that those who engage in such explorations tend to be located far from the cutting-edge experience of serfdom and alienation which gave rise to the Hebrew witness concerning Creation. The waters of Cam do not generate the same bitterness as those of Babylon. I look back over sixty-odd years of ordained ministry, and I have to acknowledge that the problem of belief for me has not been the persuasive rhetoric of those who tell us what we are made of and how our universe is structured; the problem is the weakness of our representation of the mercy of God and of God's defiant interruption on behalf of the silenced. The things which make it most difficult to believe in a good Creator remain the same as in the days of the Hebrew writers, that righteousness does not seem to triumph, that success seems to go to those who do not acknowledge that the earth is the Lord's, and who exploit it in competition with each other and lay waste its riches and its fruitfulness in greed and acquisition, that we feel ourselves to be locked in a determinism of economic and social forces from which there is no escape. In a word, our problem of belief is caused not by science but by sin. If I have faith in the Creator disclosed in the Bible, it is not because some physicists can show how their faith in God converges with their professional wisdom, but because of the character and the priorities of God and God's mandates to us. If there is any rationality in the notion of being outside the realm of measurement, if there is rationality in the notion of eternity, in due course Artificial Intelligence will find it. If there is any rationality in the notion of a Supreme Being, Artificial Intelligence will find it. (This would not necessarily prove the existence of such a Supreme Being; but, if the old ontological argument is sound, a Supreme Being which really exists is more truly a Supreme Being than one which is only a notion and not a reality.) But then, is Artificial Intelligence going to disclose the character of such a Supreme Being? That is the key question, the decisive issue. Will such intelligence define for us the God of Mercy? In the biblical story of Creation, and its climax in the Seventh Day, God is disclosed as a God who, against all the conventional power-systems of the world, is on our side, on the side of the poor, the oppressed peasant, the victim of economic fatalism, the stupid, the excluded, the ignored, the person labelled as a problem and treated as rubbish. A God who is like that is the God of the Scriptures. Any other kind of deity, however impressive, who is claimed as creator, is something else; and I will not worship.

11.

Connecting to Jesus

Cherisher, Breaker, Re-Connector of the Sabbath

This book is testimony to the incalculable blessing which Christians inherit from our Jewish ancestry. Without the theological courage of the architects of the Hebrew scriptures, the people of my area and generation would probably have nothing better to live by than a Babylonian mind-world of fatalism and oppression. Against so much evidence of disorder and cruelty in the world, Israel lived with a vision of a True God of Creation; the fruitfulness and goodness of this Creation were expressed and celebrated in the Sabbath, its purpose and its fulfilment. Christian theology takes us a stage further. Creation is fulfilled in Jesus, in the enabling of the Creator God to become part of Creation and to live in it (Colossians 1:15–20 – the almost absurd claim made concerning the bundle of flesh lying in a manger). The Word was made flesh, as the Creator's original intention, not just because things had gone wrong.

But things had gone wrong. The Sabbath had gone wrong. The life begun in Mary's womb went on to experience crucifixion. In spite of all that they had learned, the people of Israel had not been living in a continual state of wisdom and holiness. Their prophets had the difficult duty, at almost regular intervals, of pointing out their community's failure to live according to their best insights. Jesus came on the scene, as a further example of that tradition. By that time, the Jewish people had been suffering centuries of persecution, defeat and occupation by a succession of hostile forces. The promise of freedom had become obscured. Generations of prophets had warned that God would punish disobedience of the Law; the guardians of the law had become obsessed with concern for the fulfilment of the Law in scrupulous detail. As a result, Jesus found that the Sabbath had been transformed from a celebration of freedom into an instrument of repression, an obstacle to the divine purpose of healing and renewal (Luke 6:1–11; John 5:1–18). On many occasions, people approached Jesus with requests for his help as a healer; he made himself accessible to them; he responded. But when he healed on the Sabbath, this was not because anyone asked; it was at his own initiative. He offered a deliberate challenge. He was not weakening the principle of the Sabbath. He was not intervening on behalf of employers who resented the weekly pause in productivity, or on behalf of grafters who wanted to be able to go on cheating 24/7. He acted on behalf of people who were excluded on account of disability. He offered compassion to those to whom the official system gave no compassion. So, Jesus sees a woman who is crippled and he heals her, sets her free to be what she is designed to be; in so doing, he sees the Sabbath crippled; he heals the Sabbath, sets it free to be what it was designed to be (Luke 13:10–17). Jesus re-affirmed the essential character and purpose of the Sabbath, and claimed to be putting into practice the promise of the Sabbatical year of the Lord (Luke 4:18–21). He came not to destroy it but to fulfil. As a student of the inherited Law, he did not have to invent anything new. He did not even have to identify the two pre-eminent commandments, of love of God and of neighbour: a local lawyer could easily do that. But he did put those two Laws into a distinct category on their own, giving them higher authority than all the Law and the Prophets, including even the Sabbath and the Ten Commandments. So the value of all other laws has to be assessed in terms of their fulfilment of those two laws; and where that fulfilment fails, those two laws have priority.

Yes, we see Jesus as the fulfilment of the law. But anyone who reads the whole of Leviticus will see that in that book there are elements which I am not claiming as having authority, elements which some of us might wish were not there. I may be accused of cherry-picking, selecting those elements that fit my preferences and omitting the rest. It is only too easy to edit Holy Scripture to bring it into line with Political Correctness. At this point we may find that we do not see eye to eye with our Jewish cousins. We acknowledge that it is not for us to pass judgement on Holy Scripture or to bend it to suit our current opinion. But we do see Jesus as the one who judges. Jesus saw himself as fulfilling the Sabbath purposes, and for that reason we take Sabbath seriously. He affirmed the true value of Sabbath, as opposed to the ways in which the leaders of his society were using it. He claimed it as liberation, instead of restriction. He released the brake which conventional applications had put on it. So we are justified in giving priority to the Sabbath provisions in the Pentateuch, the 'law of Moses', but now with Jesus as our authority rather than Moses. With all due respect to Moses, he was not crucified for us.

Outside the Sabbath references, Jesus revised divine revelation. He 'made all foods clean' (Mark 7:19). By welcoming the touch of the woman with the haemorrhage and calling her action 'faith', he overturned an attitude of restriction which can affect half the human race (Mark 5:24–34, see Leviticus 15:19–30) – and Jairus, the man of status who was responsible for the spiritual hygiene of his community, accepted that his daughter was being touched by the healer who had just been contaminated by the touch of that nameless woman. Jesus went out of his way to overrule elements in the law which disabled rather than enabled, which penalised people on account of their sexual identity.[92]

Jesus, as a Jew, came affirming the purposes of the Creator, which are wider than the measures of the Law. In following his example, we find that there are elements of the Law which we must set aside. Whether it fits our preferences or not, we are called to take his judgement as our guide.[93]

Jesus was a Jew; and Jesus was a man. But his meaning went far beyond these identities. You do not have to be an Aramaic-speaking carpenter in order to sense that Jesus is 'one of us'. It was with a true instinct that Julian of Norwich was able to see Jesus as our beloved Mother, who feeds us on himself. 'A mother's is the most intimate, willing, and dependable of all services. None has been able to fulfil it properly but Christ and he alone can.'[94] So Julian recognises that gender-labels cannot restrict the identity of God. God, who makes human in his image as female and male, is also to be acknowledged as Mother as much as Father.

After his ministry up and down the country, Jesus came to Jerusalem, bringing with him a growing experience as a boundary-puncturer. Entering the city, he made himself accessible to the crowds, by riding on a donkey. Riding on such a beast, his eyes were no higher than the eyes of the pedestrians; his speed was such that a fairly lame walker could keep up with him. He came to another great badge of traditional identity, the Temple. Here was another institution which had been intended as a sign of God's gracious and welcoming presence; but it had become a place of limitation and exclusion. In accordance with its foundational origin, it was reserved for Jews. But it did have a feature which most Christian churches do not have, a space dedicated for nonmembers. However, it was this area of access, the Court of the Gentiles, which, in practice was cluttered with the facilities for maintaining the Temple's own economic stability. When Jesus cleared away the tables of the money-changers, he did so in order to claim the purpose of the Temple to be a 'house of prayer for all nations' (Mark 11:17). He affirmed its wider purpose. Further, he rejected the tradition, inherited from King David, that people with disabilities should be treated as outsiders. Disabilities such as blindness or lameness were seen as an indication that the Creation had gone wrong; so there should be no room for them in the place which was designed to show God's glory and his presence (2 Samuel 5:6–8). But when Jesus saw that some such people had managed to get round the rules and were there in the Temple, he welcomed them. He acted as the accessible healer, and he extended the Creator's healing purpose to those who had no right to be there. And when the Temple authorities protested against the noisy presence of children, again Jesus, far from excluding them, positively welcomed them and affirmed their noise as praise of the Creator (Matthew 21:14–16). His reclaiming of the primary intention of the Temple was part of his Gospel purpose, with the same motive as his reclaiming of the Sabbath.

In his own life and relationship, Jesus followed the pattern of Sabbath. Just as the whole story of Creation started in God and proceeded forward to God in the Seventh Day, Jesus' being begins and is fulfilled in relationship with the Father. The seventeenth chapter of John's Gospel gives us the most profound insight into Jesus' spirit. It is the very heart of the Bible. It is as if we are overhearing one half of a telephone conversation. As we are in the same room as the speaker whom we can hear, we can sense the responses and the character of the person on the other end of the line whom we cannot hear. For Jesus, the supreme fact of life was his 'abiding in' the Father. Let us recall the pattern of his relationship which we noted earlier (see page 63 above). From his 'abiding' in his eternal and immeasurable home, he actively moved out, sent into the world. Having arrived, he worked; the love that he brought from the Father worked through him, in accessibility to those who most needed to receive mercy. There, his hours and his contacts could be noted and measured and counted. But that working was not indefinitely prolonged. He moved away from it into the phase of returning and arrival, being drawn back by the accepting love of the Father, for a further stage of abiding, in the incalculable life of eternity. The acceptance was not a reward for the working; the working was the product of the abiding. It was the pattern of Jesus' whole life; but it was also a pattern that was renewed every day. The basic shape of this process, from God to God, is the fundamental motive of Creation and of Sabbath. It can be seen as a pattern of human normality. It is the pattern into which Jesus invites his disciples to follow and to share. That is how the Body of Christ is called to be, nourished by the circulation of the Blood of Christ. The pattern of Jesus is a blessing for the disciple of Jesus to claim; it is our normality. And it is a model and mandate for the whole human community.

We have seen two distinct themes in the purpose of the Sabbath: the rest, or the 'abiding', and the intervention into conventional processes on behalf of the oppressed, the debtor, the slave, and the ignorant. The Sabbath authorises the mandate which is commended by many wise spiritual advisors, to maintain a balance between 'doing' and 'being' – a mandate which is especially pertinent to ministers of religion! Jesus was supremely committed to such a double mandate. When we read of his activities, especially when he challenges the misuse of the Sabbath and defies the rules, we may get the impression that he just sails in instinctively, confident in his superior authority as Son of God. I don't think that it was like that.

There had been prophets before him, from Jeremiah to John the Baptist, who had got into trouble with the authorities. But they had not been overruling the conventions of the Law. They had not been 'numbered with the transgressors'(Isaiah 53:12); they had not got notoriety for their companionship with people who, according to the conventions of the Law, were criminals (Luke 15:1–2). It was not as a Prison Visitor that Jesus associated with 'criminals'. He was not a social scientist, making observations and gathering statistics about offenders. He belonged among them, became associated with them in their criminality. And that doesn't happen without cost, without weighing up loss in terms of one's acceptance and credibility with the People Who Matter. But Jesus was following the Sabbath motive, of intervention on behalf of People Who Don't Matter. That required more than a spontaneous gesture. That was policy and commitment. It was the product of his dedication to the other Sabbath agenda, the 'rest', the 'abiding' in the acceptance of the Father.

After his resurrection, the followers of Jesus were led by his Spirit into facing the same kind of problems and opportunities that he himself had coped with. Like Jesus, they came up against controversy concerning the significance of 'the Law'. For Paul, the main issue was not the Sabbath but the identificational symbol of circumcision. Some of his Gentile converts thought that if they took on board that identity, with all that it stood for, they would become superior Christians. For them, in a word, Christ was not enough. In the competition for getting to the top of the ladder of virtue, they wanted something more. Paul himself was an obedient Jew. Doubtless, he sang the psalms of delight in the law. He insisted that the law is holy, just, and good (Romans 7:12). But at this point, he had to denounce the appeal of 'the Law', seeing it as a pathway into loss of all that Christ has given us. He saw how 'law moves in to fill a relationship vacuum'.[95] So he demanded, 'you have been set free – don't get caught into slavery' (Galatians 5:1–4).

All down our history as Church, there have been similar attractions for making an élite of Christians who can feel superior to the common membership, taking something good and making it a device for exclusion.[96] We have come with a message of freedom, but in practice our organisation has been experienced as an instrument of control. That is unfortunate for those who are being thus controlled, but it is disastrous for those who, consciously or unconsciously, are doing the controlling. Our Lord's patience must sometimes be wearing very thin.

Jesus came as a Jew. We have no idea of his facial appearance, but perhaps he had a Jewish nose; that would have been an element of his unchosen genetic inheritance. He certainly had a Jewish penis, caused by an unchosen but consciously performed ceremony in his cultural inheritance. But, for those both inside and outside those inheritances, there is a yet more important badge or insignia. When people were devising signs for Christian identity in Sign Language with Deaf people, they had to face the vital question: How do we find a sign for 'Jesus'? There were many possibilities within the existing vocabulary – Lord, Saviour, Friend, Healer. But to recognise the central fact about Jesus, they settled for the sign of touching the palm of one hand with the middle finger of the other hand. The marks of the crucifying nails are the essential sign to identify Jesus. That is why the Apostle Thomas demanded to see them, to touch and verify them (John 20:25). He was not merely asking for evidence that Jesus was alive; he demanded evidence that the alive one had genuinely been crucified. A Saviour who had come back from such a death to life unscathed would be no saviour at all. Such a saviour would not be one of us; he would just be God in disguise; he would be a splendid specimen of divine superior technology, but not a source of hope for struggling and damaged genuine human beings. This was why Thomas demanded assurance. And so Deaf people are powerfully correct in seeing the scarred hands as the sign for 'Jesus'.

We claim that in Christ God became incarnate, and being incarnate means being at the mercy of the place where incarnation happens. In Christ God has been marked as slaves are marked, has experienced redundancy and valuelessness, has been treated as rubbish and disposable. He was rejected by the authorities of the day, both Jewish and Roman, and by the 'will of the people', public opinion. Pilate offered a local referendum. Voters had a choice; and they chose Barabbas. And so the nails were driven into his hands and feet.

Christ's resurrection was not a miraculous return to his previous life. That life had been destroyed on the cross. He genuinely died and was buried. It is, perhaps, unfortunate that in English we have followed the form of the Latin word 'resurrection'. A word beginning with 're' suggests going back – return, or reverse, or repair. What happened to Jesus was not a resuscitation of the old. It was a moving into the new being, a going forwards. The word in Greek is anastasis – standing up – 'opstanding' in Dutch and Afrikaans, 'auferstehung' in German, 'atgyfodiad' in Welsh.[97] British Sign Language has, again, got it right. The sign for 'resurrection' is to hold the left palm out flat and to plant the first two fingers of the right hand vertically upon it, like legs. 'Christ is risen' becomes a sign of powerful action.[98] Christ stands up, and moves forward into the life of eternity. The powers of death, which seek to cure problems by destruction, cannot hold him back (Acts 2:24). Christ dies because of his refusal to compromise his obedience to the Father, his insistence on the mandates of the Creator. This unlocks the potential for the bursting-forth of new life. The operations of imperial soldiery fail to imprison him. The generous attentions of faithful disciples, with their useless bags of preservative spices, fail to trap him in the place where they think that they can find him. Into eternity he moves with our humanity, retaining the scars which we humans inflict upon each other and therefore onto God. He moves into eternity; he moves also into Galilee, into the familiar place of day-to-day confusion, the border-country of unbelieving relatives and surprising strangers, the scene where the nuts and bolts of practical obedience have to be discovered and worked out. He will be there before us, and we may have to move quickly to catch up (Mark 16:7).

The life into which Christ moves is the life which he invites us to share, that is the life of the Seventh Day, stretching out to include the whole of Creation as it was begun on the First Day. It was because of his defiant insistence on the inclusive principles of the Sabbath that Jesus stirred the hostility of the authorities; he attacked its use as a boundary to God's creative renewal. The stories in the Gospels may appear to be just a series of incidents in which Jesus insisted, time and again, on the principles of the Sabbath; he was healing exclusion, interrupting the disorders which threaten community. Each incident appears to be a separate event. He meets one person after another; they come onto and off the stage, with no apparent programme or organised policy. A series of 'one-offs', of bits and pieces. But the resurrection-gospel ties them all together into a concerted witness of divine assertion of all that Sabbath was designed for. Each incident, each person, has their place. Each detail is not lost. So, at the end of his long series of glorious significances of resurrection, Paul can end by dropping right down to where we are: 'So, get on with what you are doing, put everything you have got into it, because in the Lord nothing is wasted' (1 Corinthians 15:58).

This is resurrection hope. It can make apparently fruitless

efforts worthwhile. It was a hope that enabled colleagues to stay together in the discouragements of the apartheid regime. At a time when the situation in Northern Ireland seemed to be simply getting worse and worse, the Irish poet Seamus Heaney spoke to us at a gathering of the Wilfred Owen Association in Shrewsbury. Someone asked him, 'Are you optimistic or pessimistic about Northern Ireland?' He answered, 'Optimism says, "We are going to win." Hope says, "What we are doing is worth doing." I have hope.'

Every mechanic knows 'Murphy's Law'; it states that if something can go wrong it will go wrong. If you find that a door is shut against you, you may well have another door slammed in your face. There is a kind of religion which tells us, Trust in God and say your prayers, and what you are afraid of will not happen. The faith of the disciples of Jesus will answer, Yes, trust in God and say your prayers and quite possibly the thing that you are most afraid of will happen; but when it does, you will find that it is not something to be afraid of. At the time of writing this, our whole world is caught by a fence of fear, which both unites us and divides. We knew something like this during World War II, especially in the first 18 months, when everything was going wrong. My school, on vulnerable Merseyside, was evacuated to rural Wales – which was okay for us children but left us deeply afraid that we might never see our parents and home again. There were times in South Africa when we were almost paralysed by fear of what the Security Police was doing to us. Later, we found ourselves trapped in Britain, unable to return to home, friends and employment, and that was a long and painful test of confidence. But, time and again, we find that the God who is God of eternity has a limitless stock of Second Chances. And now I find that both my wife and myself are classified as 'vulnerable'. So, what next? Mother Julian of Norwich is well-known for her quotation of what Jesus said to her: 'All shall be well and all shall be well, and all manner of thing shall be well.'[99] We need to remember that, in the voice of both Jesus and Julian, these words are not just an optimistic truism. Faced with the realities of sin and evil, she had a big struggle to accept this message. It was not simply that God's in his heaven and all is right with the world. The message became true for her because she had seen so deeply into the pain and trial of the death of Christ, affirming that the love of God our Father and Mother is stronger than all else; or, as I have quoted from our Iona Prayer Book, we believe in God's goodness at the heart of humanity, planted more deeply than all that is wrong. It is the crucified, living, resurrected, Christ who has the authority to make such a statement. That sort of resurrection-faith transforms even death: death can become not a departure but an arrival.[100] Let us recall the witness of Dietrich Bonhoeffer. Imprisoned by the Nazis, certain of facing eventual death at their hands, an execution which actually took place just a few weeks before the end of World War II in Europe, Bonhoeffer could claim: 'Death is the supreme festival on the road to freedom.'[101] For him, freedom and death belonged together.

If we claim Christ's company when we 'tread the verge of Jordan', we do so as people who are committed to Christ's purpose of freedom. I have already referred to a friend for whom the 'river' – in her case the River Ohio – had special meaning. Let me tell of another friend, and of another river. Eva had been born in Germany, in about 1930, of Jewish parents; she was one of those children who escaped into Britain just before World War II. She became a Christian, trained as a teacher, and was sent by a missionary society to work with the church in India. From there she moved to similar work in Kenya, where she was in the thick of the terror and danger of the Mau Mau uprising. She returned to Britain and became the pioneer Chaplain for Overseas Students in Manchester. In that role she attended a conference in Leeds in 1963, which I also attended when my family and I were on a three-month visit to UK. A few years later, she came to South Africa, to put her huge experience and wisdom to work for education and support for black people whose education had been wrecked by the apartheid regime. This was to be her life's work, and she brought a wonderful resource of hope and energy into a deeply depressing situation. At the height of her vigour and vision, she was suddenly struck down by an inoperable cancer. To avoid being a drain on precious resources, she felt that she had to move back to Britain, to die. She was one of the first people to stay in Cicely Saunders' pioneer hospice in London. My wife Shirley and I saw her several times as she got steadily weaker. Inevitably, she was wondering what God was up to – just as I was, having what I thought was my life's work suddenly cancelled by the South African government. On our last visit to her, she started to tell us, with great difficulty in speech, and with her face a leaden jaundice colour, about a vision which she had just experienced. She was standing on a river bank. On the opposite side there was a great crowd of people, mainly African, who had been through trials and disasters, and were encouraging her to come across. They had built up a great credit-balance of faith, a treasury of courage, which they were offering for her to draw on. As she was describing this vision, her voice became strong and familiar, her face resumed its usual colour, and it was as if herself had been given back to her. A couple of hours later, she made the crossing; she arrived.

The communion of saints is the community of solidarity in freedom, a fellowship of support in pilgrimage; so, like the slaves at the Ohio, we are not alone in our crossing. Christ is Risen; 'death of death and hell's destruction, land me safe on Canaan's side'. What we are doing is worth doing.

Where Jesus met people who saw the point of what he was

doing, he called it 'faith'. Mostly, they were people who were on the receiving end of the ways in which the guardians of the law were using the law to exclude. They were being excluded on account of their infirmity or poverty or cultural identity or gender. He saw the potential in people who were otherwise seen only as problems. He comes as liberator, overcoming boundaries of wealth and status. Conventional society congratulates the powerful on being powerful, conventional wisdom congratulates the clever on being clever, conventional religion congratulates good people on being good. The Gospel of Jesus says, Congratulations to you, you who don't belong anywhere, you who are reckoned as stupid or disabled, you who are morally mixed-up. You are made in the image of God, who sees God's own face in yours. God's son is your brother, who wants no honour for himself as long as his sisters and brothers are dishonoured. And you don't have to do anything to prove it.

Jesus is our Redeemer, affirming the ancient intention of God for all creation, human and non-human; he still comes to deliver the universe from mercilessness. He calls his disciples in every age to share in that ageless purpose. The truth of this God is not tested in argument or point-scoring. This God is the one with whom we can stay faithful in the darkness of Babylon, because he has shown that he will stay faithful to us. We do not merely talk about this God, but we obey, we worship. And with this God we can rest, content to follow our unique calling to be borderers, to inhabit the country where matter and spirit meet and march together. The darkness is punctuated by God's mercy, the mercy of the Seventh Day.

Alleluia: the earth is the Lord's. And all that is in it.

Christ is Risen: he is risen indeed. Alleluia.

Notes and References

At a time when I was a confused student, unsuccessfully trying to get my head around some German philosophy, I was delighted to pick up the following gem-like truism, the opening sentence of an old 'Walsingham Pilgrim's Manual': '*There is a connection between everything and everything else, pilgrimages not excepted.*' I love that jump from the universal to the particular – worthy of the Doctrine of the Incarnation. And you can try substituting anything that you like for the word 'pilgrimages' – scampi, aunts, trigonometry, Eisteddfodau, Wing Commanders, urine, scalpels, semiquavers, USBs, magpies... The following section of this book is a conglomeration of academic linkages and personal oddities. I offer that quotation as a dedication and introduction to these miscellaneous Notes, on a book that is all about connections.

For the reference for the quotation from David Jones on the title-page, see note 33 below. The two lines following are the opening lines of the first poem, in Welsh and English, which Grahame Davies, poet and teacher in Cardiff, wrote in response to an invitation from the Prince of Wales to celebrate the Llangollen International Musical Eisteddfod. These poems were published in *A World in Harmony* (Llangollen, Eisteddfod Office, 2004). Dr Davies is himself a borderer, born in Coedpoeth, Wrexham. Literal English version of the first line in Welsh is: 'The border can be a place of meeting or a place of No Exit.' I am grateful to Dr Davies for his agreement to my quotation of his words in this context.

CHAPTER ONE

[1] Dietrich Bonhoeffer, *Creation and Fall* (London, SCM Press 1959), 41.

[2] 'It would be several decades before any major composer (i.e. Wagner) would go further in chromatic ambiguity than Haydn did' at this point. Nicholas Temperley, *Haydn: The Creation* (Cambridge, CUP 1991), 83.

CHAPTER TWO

[3] At this point, I recall a story of a musician who, at a rehearsal of a symphony by Vaughan Williams, had doubts about the accuracy of a certain note in his score. As the composer happened to be present, the player took the opportunity of a pause in the proceedings to go to the great man and ask, very hesitantly, 'This B natural here, surely ought it not to be a B flat?' VW checked it very carefully and answered, 'It looks wrong and it sounds wrong; but it's right.' True for the theological biology of Genesis – and of quite a lot of other mysteries in our faith (Story quoted in Bernard Shore, *The Orchestra Speaks* (London, Longmans Green 1938)).

[4] Viktor Frankl, *Man's Search for Meaning* (London, Rider 2004), 80.

[5] Seán Morrow, *The Fires Beneath: The Life of Monica Wilson, South African Anthropologist* (Cape Town, Penguin Books 2016), 265.

[6] John L. Bell, *Living with the Psalms* (London, SPCK 2020), 121.

[7] Yet, in spite of this, in the church where I was a curate sixty years ago, we spent several meetings weighing up the apparently heretical question as to whether it would be proper to celebrate the Maundy Thursday Mass in the evening.

[8] I have a lot of sympathy for those crafty warriors who were supposed to be guarding the tomb. As an Airframes Fitter in the RAF, in 1947 I was stationed for several months on an airfield where there were a couple of hundred redundant warplanes slowly rotting away, parked on the grass. Every night, a pair of us was detailed to be on guard over these derelict machines. We assumed, first, that only a somewhat stupid officer could have set up such a pointless routine, and, secondly, that if some idiot did get in among these scrapyard antiques with evil intent then, equipped as we were with one torch and no batteries, there was

not much that we could do about it. So, after dutifully walking around the airfield for an hour, we would climb into a convenient Halifax and curl up and go to sleep. The Garden Guard on Holy Saturday might well have had a similar angle on their duties.

[9] I offer a bit more detail about this experience at note 93.

[10] John M. Hull, *In the Beginning there was Darkness* (London, SCM Press 2001), 142.

[11] See John D. Davies, *Be Born in us Today* (Norwich, The Canterbury Press 1999), 137–155.

[12] John Habgood, *Varieties of Unbelief* (London, Darton, Longman and Todd 2000) 116f.

CHAPTER THREE

[13] Jonathan Sacks, *The Great Partnership* (London, Hodder & Stoughton 2011), 130.

[14] For an extended and authoritative exposition of this theme, see Michael Northcott, *A Moral Climate* (London, Darton, Longman and Todd 2007).

CHAPTER FOUR

[15] Jenifer M. Baker, *A Theological Enquiry into the Processes of Painting* (Doctoral Thesis for York St John University 2017), p.45. Dr Baker is a biologist, (an internationally-recognised authority on the effects of maritime oil-spills), a painter, and a priest of the Church of England. I am glad to acknowledge her advice and support in the writing of the present book.

[16] Robert W. Jenson, *Systematic Theology 2 The Works of God* (Oxford, OUP 2001).

[17] I'm sorry, but I have no idea of where, in his extensive writings, Dr van Loon says this. But I remember it clearly, almost from my mother's knee (she was a teacher of art) and it has stuck with me all my life.

[18] See T. H. White's account of Merlin's lecture to the future King Arthur, recounting the Creator's mandate to the first man: 'Man, you

will be a naked tool all your life, though a user of tools. You will look like an embryo until they bury you, but all others will be embryos before your might; eternally undeveloped, you will always remain *potential* in Our image.' T. H. White, *The Sword in the Stone* (London, Collins 1950), 314.

[19] As the old adage says, 'She walks with a wiggle because her children are so clever.' When our cartoonists depict clever persons, and especially evil clever persons, they give them skulls which could not possibly be delivered by a human mother.

[20] 'For 99% of human history, unless our ancestors had committed murder and adultery we wouldn't be here today.' Adrian Bailey, *Why Darwin Matters to Christians,* (Shrewsbury, YouCaxton Publications 2011), 40

[21] Saint Augustine *Confessions:* translated by R. S. Pine-Coffin (Harmondsworth, Penguin 1961), 28.

[22] John Burnaby, *Darwin and the Human Situation* (Cambridge, W. Heffer 1959), 10.

[23] Julian Huxley, *Evolution in Action* (New York, Harper 1953), 146.

[24] T. H. Huxley, *Evolution and Ethics* (New York, D. Appleton 1896), 83. See Ian Barbour, *Issues in Science and Religion* (London, SCM Press 1966), 408–414.

[25] Richard Dawkins, *The Selfish Gene* (Oxford, OUP 1989), 200–201.

[26] Pope Francis, *Encyclical Letter Laudate Si'* (Rome, Libreria Editrice Vaticana 2015), paragraph 224.

[27] Manon Ceridwen James, *Women, Identity and Religion in Wales* (Cardiff, University of Wales Press 2018), 100.

[28] Julian of Norwich, *Revelations of Divine Love,* (trans. Clifton Wolters, Harmondsworth, Penguin 1966), 84, 181.

[29] As a child, I often felt stupid at my failure to understand the laughter of my elders. But there came an occasion when I found for myself something which seemed to me – and still seems to me – to be absurdly funny. It was a sentence in a newspaper, as follows: 'In order to prove his dominance and masculinity, Major X threw a cardboard clock-face at the wall.' I found this

when I was about 14 and was just signing up to the Army Cadets. The kind of humour of resistance which Dr James identifies was a vital resource for us during the apartheid years in South Africa. An example: Scene – a city street, with a bench labelled "Slegs vir Blankes (For White Persons Only)". On the bench lie, with empty bottles, two shabby white men, obviously drunk and incapable. Two respectably-dressed black men are passing by, carrying briefcases. One says to the other, "Look, my brother: voters.'" Humour can nourish defiance.

[30] Manon Ceridwen James, *op.cit.,* 110.

[31] John D. Davies, *Three Mountains to Freedom* (Blandford Forum, Deo Publishing 2016), 54.

CHAPTER FIVE

[32] Philip Newell, *The Book of Creation* (Norwich, Canterbury Press 1999), 84.

[33] David Jones, essay *Art and Democracy* in *Epoch and Artist* (London, Faber and Faber 1959), 86.

[34] See note 15 above.

[35] I live in a parish about three miles from the border between Wales and England. Although it is authoritatively in Shropshire, the electricity supply company gives me proper warning against misbehaviour, by a placard on the supply pole, proclaiming 'Peidiwch â dringo' ('Don't climb'). I appreciative the recognition. And we are profoundly grateful for remarkable advantages in relating to two different areas of the Health Service.

[36] Several years ago, I put together a short text (about 26,000 words) of how eight of the great Gospel themes (creation, redemption, trinity, etc.) could speak to different groups or churches, according to whether they were rural or suburban or town centre. This was not published; but if anyone would like to see it, please get in touch. It is called 'Three Angles on the Gospel'. The distinction between 'local' and 'cosmopolitan' was worked out in detail by our Sociology professor at Keele, Ronald Frankenberg (*Communities in Britain* (Harmondsworth, Penguin 1960)).

[37] Claiming the ancient Celtic vision that there are places where heaven is only three feet away from earth.

[38] From a personal letter from a representative of the orthodox Chabad movement in Israel, by courtesy of Mrs Sylvia Gefen of Tel Aviv.

[39] Werner Pelz, *Irreligious Reflections on the Christian Church* (London, SCM Press 1959), 77.

[40] There is, perhaps, a slight irony in the fact that dutiful Christian worshippers expect God to take most notice of us on his rest-day. I was a novice Prison-Visitor for a time in the 1950s; I used regularly to visit a rather unsuccessful con-man called Doug, who didn't hold with Sunday services in the prison, because, as he said, 'Sunday is God's day-off'. Muslims may be wiser – God is always on duty on Friday.

[41] Frank Lake, *Clinical Theology* (London, Darton, Longman and Todd, 1966), 140.

[42] Niemöller was a close friend of Dietrich Bonheoffer in leadership of the Confessing Church in Germany under Nazism. Bonhoeffer was hanged a few weeks before the end of World War II; Niemöller survived, and was the most inspiring and influential of many ecumenical visitors who came to us in South Africa during the apartheid regime.

[43] In the diagram which accompanies the text at this point, the design of the square represents the four-fold process which Dr Lake offers as pattern of human normality; key moments of change are marked by asterisks at B and D, when we Go Out and Return. The text on the inside of the diagram relates this to the history of Jesus. W. H. Vanstone, in *The Stature of Waiting* (London, Darton, Longman and Todd, 1982), p.20ff, recalls the experience (which strongly coincides with my own) of how being hospitalised takes one from doing to being-done-to, and being subject to other people's timing. Rachel Mann, in *Fierce Imaginings* (London, Darton, Longman and Todd, 2017), p.55, shows how a similar change is to be seen in the image of the soldier in the Great War. Given to us by poets such as David Jones and Wilfred Owen, our picture of 'the soldier' is no longer that of a splendidly-attired swordsman on horseback but a khaki-clad struggler half-buried in mud and guts.

[44] Philip Newell, *op. cit.* 102. I once knew a priest who was highly regarded as a counsellor and source of wisdom. He used to say: 'If I wake up and I am in pyjamas, it's time for Mass. If I wake up and I am fully dressed, it's time for tea.' In real achievement, this apparently dormouse character was more valued than many more obviously activist colleagues.

CHAPTER SIX

[45] Figures from the Clewer Initiative, under the authority of the Archbishops' Council of the Church of England. This information warns us to recognise that, while there may be a lot of energy and enthusiasm for removing statues of the enslavers of past history, slavery is still part of our contemporary world, and not just in distant lands. The COVID-19 virus pandemic has exposed vulnerable people to exploitation, in occupations which are weakly regulated, for instance those which have been caught in the rush to produce large quantities of protective equipment such as face masks. And farmers and fruit-growers can discover that they have unwittingly been supplied with unlicensed workers, exploited by irresponsible agencies who criminally ignore the rules about workers' rights (see the Modern Slavery Helpline – www. theclewerinitiative.org Farm Work Welfare app).

[46] John Rogerson (ed.), *Leviticus in Practice* (Blandford Forum, Deo, 2014), 14.

[47] Mark Scarlata, *Sabbath Rest: The Beauty of God's Rhythm for a Digital Age* (London, SCM Press 2019), p.90f.

[48] See Viktor Frankl, *Man's Search for Meaning,* 74.

[49] Lesslie Newbigin, *The Welfare State: A Christian Perspective,* in *Theology* (London, SPCK May 1985), 181.

[50] Justin Welby, *Dethroning Mammon* (London, Bloomsbury 2015), 146ff.

For some first-century Christians, 'Babylon' was Rome, the crucifying, colonising domination system that stole wealth from the poor to the advantage of the privileged. Rome enriched itself with the commodities produced by the dedicated labour of religious servants of the Lord. Dr Welby quotes the whole of Revelation 18, with the central list of commodities with which the city had enriched itself, a list which echoes the depredations suffered by Israel in their Babylonian captivity. In his passionate oratorio 'Belshazzar's Feast' (the first piece of big music which really spoke to me as a teenager), William Walton includes this list, with ironic accent, as it moves from mineral wealth to animal wealth to its climax in 'slaves – and the souls of men'. We humans are ourselves victims of the domination system, traded in its mechanisms. Walton's music testifies to the cruelty and greed of the domination system, and to the system's fragility and its collapse. It is powerful as an interpretation of the old text, but doubly powerful if we hear it for our own day, as the Christians of Rome heard of 'Babylon' for their own day. Ultimately, the merchandising of things and of people is doomed; the domination system will not prevail over the values of God's Kingdom. For this we pray day by day, as instructed by our Master.

[51] John Milton sonnet, *On his arrival at the age of twenty-three.*

CHAPTER SEVEN

[52] Julius Nyerere, *Freedom and Unity* (Dar es Salaam, OUP 1974), 53.

[53] For a detailed and poignant example of how this process affected one family, the ancestral family of the present Archbishop of Capetown, see Thabo Makgoba, *Faith and Courage* (London, SPCK 2019), pp.3–15.

[54] From Submission to Enquiry into proposed super quarry affecting Roineabhal Mountain, by the Rev. Professor Donald MacLeod.

[55] For thorough exposition of this theme, based mainly on Leviticus 25, see Frederick Verinder, *My Neighbour's Landmark* (London, Land and Liberty Press 1950). Also John D. Davies *The Earth is the Lord's* in John Rogerson (ed.), *Leviticus in Practice* (Blandford Forum, Deo Publishing 2014).

[56] *The Bible in Transmission, Summer 2016* (Swindon, The Bible Society 2016).

[57] From a speech by Dr Michael Hudson of Harvard, at Union Theological Seminary, Columbia, on 23 January 2017.

[58] From an unpublished lecture by Dr King at St Louis in 1964, a recording of which, with his blessing, a group of us distributed in South Africa in 1966, where it was immediately banned by the apartheid government. In this country there is one copy of our original recording on LP in Edinburgh, and there is another which I have given to Gladstone's Library, Hawarden.

[59] William Temple, *Christianity and Social Order* (Harmondsworth, Penguin 1942), 87. It is arguable that the neglect of this sort of critique has led to the stratospheric rise in land values in areas such as Kensington and Chelsea, the location of the Grenfell Tower.

[60] Fred Harrison, *The Traumatised Society* (London, Shepheard-Walwyn 2012), 39.

[61] *Memorandum to the Prime Minister on Unaffordable Housing* (London, Zacchaeus 2000 Trust 2005). An exceptionally well-documented and practical study, which raises the question, What has happened to it? In 2017, the Labour Party published its Manifesto; in it, on page 86, it faintly suggested that the party might consider setting up a policy of land-value taxation. Not much more than a minor hint, but it was enough to inspire some sounds of alarm from certain other quarters. And this was not repeated in the 2019 Manifesto.

[62] Henry George, *Progress and Poverty* (London, J. M. Dent 1897), 288. For an authoritative exposition of the connexions between the Hebrew Scriptures, Henry George, and our current situation, see Robert V. Andelson and James M. Dawsey, *From Wasteland to Promised Land* (London, Shepheard-Walwyn 1992).

[63] Alanna Hartzog, *The Earth Belongs to Everyone* (Radford, Virginia, The Institute for Economic Democracy Press 2008), pp.99ff.

[64] Howard J. Hammerton, *This Turbulent Priest* (London, Lutterworth Press 1952), 75, 107. Jenkinson ought to honoured as a hero of the Church and of British society. He is certainly a hero of mine – one of his estates was where my wife grew up.

[65] Equality and Human Rights Commission, *Housing and Disabled People,* 2018.

[66] Fred Harrison, *The Traumatised Society,* 30–45.

[67] Alanna Hartzog, *The Earth Belongs to Everyone,* 95.

[68] There are several places where this contrast can be seen. I have in mind a place right on the Marches border, Skenfrith in Monmouthshire – a village and church which have seen more than their fair share of the floods of February 2020.

The Church may find other occasions to sing a different song. For me, in the last public ceremony that I performed as a bishop, it was a true privilege that it took place not in a cathedral, nor in a village church, but on an open field. I acted to represent the Bishop of St Asaph in consecrating a piece of land as a public graveyard. I had several times performed such a ceremony when I was Bishop of Shrewsbury, but this was special for me, as it was for the community in Mid-Wales where I had once been Vicar, so I knew several of the citizens who were requesting this ceremony. I stood at the corners of the piece of land, marked them with the Cross, using the Episcopal crozier that the people of the church had given to me when I was consecrated Bishop, using the ancient claim, 'The earth is the Lord's' – 'Eiddo'r Arglwydd yw'r ddaear a'i llawnder'. This ceremony, in which the Minister of the Chapels of the Valley shared, under the authority of the local Council, affirms in perpetuity that the land belongs to the citizens of the place, proof against any schemes of private developers or road-wideners or mineral exploiters. It is a special responsibility of the Church to consecrate. But, when we consecrate, whether it be of things (like water, bread, or wine), or of people, or of land, we are not saying, 'These are holy, and the others are not holy,' we are saying, 'These are holy, representing the holiness of all the other things – bread, land, people, of their category.' So, when we consecrate a piece of ground, we are making a statement about all other ground around. The land which you claim as yours is only yours on loan. The earth remains the Lord's. It has the Lord's sign upon it.

CHAPTER EIGHT

[69] Pope Francis, Encyclical, para 49.

[70] Winston Halapua, *Waves of God's Embrace* (Norwich, Canterbury Press 2008), 77.

[71] Lord Rees, writing in the 'I' newspaper, 1 September 2017.

[72] Winston Halapua, *Ibid.* 92.

[73] T. S. Eliot, *Collected Poems, 1909–1935* (London, Faber & Faber 1936), 157.

[74] Our worthy Sergeant-Instructor didn't mention that, if the oleo-leg was doing what it was designed to do as part of the undercarriage of a heavy bomber, and that bomber was taking off to do the things that it was designed to do, then a whole lot of other poor buggers were likely to be killed. But that, of course was not his responsibility, nor ours.

[75] One Easter morning, I rose at 5.00 a.m, to take part in the Lighting of the New Fire for the dawn Eucharist; it was at a large city-centre church. For the amount of darkness that we had in which to kindle the visible new light, we might as well have started the service at midday.

[76] David Jones, *The Sleeping Lord* (London, Faber and Faber 1974), 62f.

[77] Dietrich Bonhoeffer, *Ethics* (London, SCM Press 1955), 329.

[78] See John D. Davies. A *Song for Every Morning – Dedication and Defiance with St Patrick's Breastplate* (Norwich, Canterbury Press 2008), 49ff.

[79] Elias Chacour, *Faith Beyond Despair: Building Hope in the Holy Land* (Norwich, Canterbury Press 2008), 114. My first experience of racism happened when I was about 12 years old, in 1938–9; my parents gave refuge to a family of four Austrian Jews, who had managed to get out of Germany; the young man had been in the concentration camp at Dachau. The way they were treated by the British authorities, and the hostility shown to my parents, taught me the meaning of the word anti-Semitism. So now it is particularly tragic when we are accused of anti-Semitism when we protest against Israel's treatment of Palestinians.

[80] Dr Michael Hudson of Harvard.

CHAPTER NINE

[81] Marin Luther, *Commentary on St Paul's Epistle to the Galatians* 1535 (London, James Clarke 1953), pp.483ff.

[82] Ann Pettifor, *The Case for the Green New Deal* (London, Verso 2019), p.124. Go to this work for an up-to-date, sophisticated, and radical analysis and interpretation of our present economic and environmental crisis. See also the same author's *The Production of Money – How to Break the Power of Bankers* (Verso 2017) and *The Coming First World Debt Crisis* (Basingstoke, Palgrave Macmillan 2006) And see Justin Welby, *Dethroning Mammon* (London, Bloomsbury 2016) and *Reimagining Britain* (London, Bloomsbury 2018); and Ron Ferguson, *George MacLeod* (Glasgow, Wild Goose Publications 2001).

[83] Josephus, *The Antiquities of the Jews* 4.8.225 and 3.12.283–284 (Josephus, *The Complete Works* (Nashville, Nelson 1998), 140 and 116).

[84] Gerd Theissen, *The Shadow of the Galilean* (London, SCM Press 1987), 62, quoting Diodorus Siculus.

[85] Archbishop Elias Chacour, *Faith Beyond Despair* (Norwich, Canterbury Press 2008), 9–11.

[86] St Ambrose, quoted, together with similar statements from the Fathers, in Kenneth Leech, *True Prayer* (London, Sheldon Press 1980), 88ff. See also Charles Avila, *Ownership. Early Christian Teachings* (Maryknoll, Orbis Books 1983) p.8, quoted in Alanna Hartzog, op.cit. p.93.

[87] Pelagius, *On Riches*, quoted in Philip Newell, *The Book of Creation*, 41.

[88] See note 46, above.

[89] See note 58.

[90] Julian of Norwich *op. cit.* 130.

[91] See Thabo Makgoba *op. cit.* pp.143ff, 215ff etc.

CHAPTER ELEVEN

[92] Mark 5:21–43. This great complex story, of two episodes interrelating with and affecting each other, yields at least 44 connections of contrast and interaction, of meaning and effect, and of response from Jesus; it is almost a summary of Jesus' ministry of healing by means of overruling the conventions of 'the Law'. See John D. Davies, *Only Say the Word* (Norwich, Canterbury Press 2002), pp.88ff.

[93] In Chapter 2 of this book, I mentioned a defining occasion in my life, when I was made aware of the presence of the Risen Christ alongside me, and alongside other people who were experiencing confusion or despair. At that time, I was a young man, confident and content in a 'normal' heterosexual identity. As a law-abiding Christian citizen, I was repelled by the sin and crime that was then referred to as 'unnatural vice', recognising the duty of the police to 'stamp it out'. Then I became friendly with two or three other men of my age, who were better and wiser and more generously Christian than I, and who were trying to make what they could of their lives as homosexual people. The law of the land was based on Leviticus 18:22. The law of the land at that time judged that any sexual act between men was criminal. I was a novice Prison Visitor, and in that role I met several men (including some clergymen) who were in prison for behaviour which would have been accepted as normal between people in two-sex relationships. So these friends of mine were criminals, and if you are a friend of criminals you become complicit in their criminality. It was really impossible for a young homosexual man, with a young person's yearning for closeness and affection, not to be a criminal. But the homosexual underworld was a world of suspicion, betrayal, blackmail, police harassment and intimidation, and suicide. (This was all before the Wolfenden Report and the decriminalisation of the relevant laws. This was about relationships between consenting adults – nothing whatever to do with abuse of minors.). I knew little about theology or ethics, but I had been accepted as a potential candidate for ordination, and I felt very ill-equipped to

deal with such a situation. With the law of both church and state being clearly condemning, there was no one that I could turn to in either law or church or medicine. That was where I was, when I was made aware of the presence of Christ alongside me; I have no doubt that this was authentically Christ present – I had neither the language or the imagery in my memory from which such a message could have crept in via my subconscious. It was gift – not even a response to prayer. From this, I eventually derived a somewhat simplistic formula, that it is better to break the rules for the sake of love than to insist on keeping the rules in order to avoid the claims of love. Simplistic, yes; but not too far from the style of Jesus in his dealing with the Sabbath rules. However, if I had told this story in my cv or at job-interviews, I would not have had much chance as a reverend; and no one who could be embarrassed by what I have said here is still alive in this world. Archbishop Makgoba's story of his life growing up in the townships of Johannesburg shows how, on a much wider scale, it was impossible for a young black South African to avoid being a criminal. Same kind of world.

[94] Julian *op. cit.* 169.

[95] David Brown, *Leaven: The Hidden Power of Culture in the Church* (Weybridge, RoperPenberthy Publishing 2016), 93. Captain Brown speaks from his experience of 34 years as a naval officer and 12 years as PA to a diocesan bishop.

[96] see John D. Davies, *Three Mountains to Freedom*, 77–85.

[97] There is, at this point, a curiously misleading and intrusive word in the English versions of the Apostles' Creed and the 'Nicene' Creed, namely the word 'again', 'he rose again'. Later in the Creed, this word means simply that Jesus will do, for a further time, what he has already done once, namely he will come to this world. In the Easter story, at this point, the 'again' seems to have two possible meanings. It could have its normal meaning of 'repeat' – as in 'I visited Finland in 1996, and again in 2007, and I intend to go there again next year'. So at this point, it could mean that Jesus had previously done some sort of 'rising' and now has done it again. But this would be contrary to the Gospel

story. Or it could have the meaning of 'resume', as in 'I fell off my motorbike when it skidded on black ice, I got up (same word as 'rose') *again,* got on the bike *again,* and resumed my journey.' But this also is not what the Gospel tells us. The risen Jesus did not continue where he had left off; his life after he got up was a fundamentally new life, not a resuscitated old life, not the kind of life which might, later on in history, have been organised for the benefit of a few people with lots of spare money to invest in deep freezing and self-preservation. The little word 'again' weakens the narrative. It has no justification in the Gospel; it does not appear in languages other than English, but it has been in English Prayer Books at least since 1549. So this is not a theological problem but a problem in language and liturgy. Perhaps a responsible theologian could start a campaign for the abolition of this word from our Easter confessions of faith.

[98] We affirm 'Christ rose from the dead'. That is correct, but the fundamental New Testament word is 'Christ is risen'. He does not raise himself. He does not have some sort of self-raiser built into his constitution. His death is as complete as yours or mine. The key phrase in the Scripture is 'Christ was raised...'. The resurrection was God's action, the Father's glorifying, the Creator's final affirmation. Similarly at the Ascension, Jesus did not take off into the sky powered by his own engine; he was 'lifted up' (Acts 1:9).

[99] Julian of Norwich, *op. cit.,* 103f.

[100] I owe this insight to my mother, who, when planning an inscription for the grave of my father and herself, demanded that the date of death should be stated not as 'departed' but as 'arrived'.

[101] Dietrich Bonhoeffer, *Letters and Papers from Prison* (London, SCM Press 1953), p.176. I rejoice to have Bonhoeffer's words as the first and last quotations in this essay. This was not part of my original plan, but it is a humble acknowledgement of an immense sense of debt.

In addition to works noted above, the following studies have been helpful to me in preparing this book:

Walter Brueggemann, *The Land* (Philadelphia, Fortress Press 1977). Essential to my argument at many points.

Jose P. Miranda, *Marx and the Bible: A Critique of the Philosophy of Oppression* (New York, Orbis 1974).

Jürgen Moltmann, *God in Creation* (Minneapolis, Fortress Press 1985).

Gordon Mursell, *Praying in Exile* (London, Darton, Longman and Todd 2005).

Simon Oliver, *Creation: A Guide for the Perplexed* (London, Bloomsbury 2017).

John Polkinghorne, *Science and Christian Belief* (London, SPCK 1994), and other works by the same authority.

Christopher J. H. Wright, *Living as the People of God* (Leicester, IVP 1983).

Tom Wright, *God and the Pandemic* (London, SPCK 2020).

Quarterly *Land and Liberty* published in London since 1894.

Acknowledgements

My wife Shirley, has, for 63 years, been my source of cherishing and inspiration. When I have been speaking with young clergy, I have said something like this: 'If you're thinking of getting married, do choose someone who is further to the left than you are. As a professional minister, you will be representing an institution; you need to have at your side someone who can remind you that before it ever became an institution, the church was a movement, and that's what it still is, with you as just an ordinary member. You will need someone who can be a critical and encouraging voice, someone who can help you to avoid getting too much tied up with the Establishment.' That, plus so much else, has been the huge support that Shirley has given me. She has been a source of encouragement and correction, in the production of the present book.

I have been ordained as deacon, priest, and bishop in the Church of England, with an English background and education (with three years in Wales during World War II, when my school was evacuated from Merseyside to havens across the border). I make no apology for this. But Shirley and I are immensely grateful to the Church in Southern Africa for giving us 15 years of another culture and sharing in its struggles. In our vocation, we should still be there, because we were forced out by the South African Government in 1970, and so are exiles in Britain. But God is indeed the God of the Second Chance; and we, with our children, give thanks that, like many other migrants, we have found a home in this country. Further, I am thankful also to the Church in Wales, and successive Bishops of St Asaph, for many further years of discovery in the Land of My Fathers.

I am grateful for the opportunity to express appreciation for the inspiration given by The Anglican Students' Federation of South Africa. I mention just four people who represent many hundreds of dedicated and courageous students. Nyameko Barney Pityana was one who was imprisoned during the apartheid regime; he became President of the University of Cape Town, and he memorably was preacher at my consecration as a Bishop in Westminster Abbey. Steve Hayes was for years, as a student and then as a priest, placed under a banning order. He is now a Reverend Deacon in the Orthodox Church in Tshwane/Pretoria, a theologian and novelist, and has been a regular correspondent with us for sixty years. Ann Pettifor's contribution as radical economist and environmental activist and leader of programmes such as Jubilee 2000 and Operation Noah, has been noted in these pages; she was first known to us as Ann Potgieter, student from the Afrikaner heartland of the Orange Free State. And there was the supremely inspiring Steve Biko, who was cruelly done to death by the Special Branch, and who would have, in my view, become the natural successor to President Nelson Mandela. All these have influenced the writing of this book.

For their advice and support, I specially thank David Wilbourne, formerly Assistant Bishop of Llandaff, Mike Bourke, formerly Bishop of Wolverhampton, Barbara Leonard, formerly Housing Manager for a Local Authority in the North-West of England, and Adrian Bailey, former Vicar and Hospital Chaplain at Selattyn and Gobowen. Gladstone's Library, Hawarden, and its resourceful Warden, Peter Francis, have, for many years, been an

Acknowledgements

unfailing storehouse of wisdom and of learned conversation, and I am grateful for this opportunity to acknowledge.

This book would not have been produced but for the enthusiasm and professional care, in exceptionally difficult times, of David Moloney, Editorial Director of Darton, Longman and Todd, and his colleagues. Sincere thanks and appreciation for their enterprises.

I am deeply grateful for the sensitive perceptions of John Bell in the Foreword which he has provided for the book. He is well-known across the world for the songs and hymns, words and music, which he, with his colleagues in the Wild Goose Worship Group, has contributed to our worship, and for his role as ambassador for Iona and our inheritance of spiritual insight. It is a great privilege for me to have his support.

Questions

Many questions are touched on in this short book, far too many to be listed. But, for individual thought and for groups to engage with, here are a few suggestions.

1. What, for you, has been the most useful point in the book? And what has been the most unhelpful or most untrue for you?

2. What were the main feelings which led your thoughts during the coronavirus pandemic? What do you feel about it now, in retrospect? Are there, for you, any connections between these feelings and the book?

3. What, for you, are the most difficult problems in believing in God as good Creator (chapters 3 to 4, and 10).

4. Is your work something which you can offer to God? Can you suggest ways in which your local Harvest Thanksgiving can be made more inclusive and involving? (Chapter 6)

5. What kind of home do you have, in terms of your rights of ownership, or rental, or occupation? How do you feel about this? How far do you experience the housing crisis of Britain? How valuable is the ideal that we should be a property-owning democracy? (Chapter 7)

6. What kind of learning have you experienced since leaving school? Has this been good and/or useful? How far, for you, has the Church been a place of learning – as opposed to just

being a place to keep a programme existing? (Chapter 8)

7. Can the ideals of Sabbath be effective in Britain? Can Sabbath and Babylon work together? (Chapter 9)

8. What responsibilities can you, and your Church, undertake in response to the challenges of climate change? (Chapters 3 and 8)

9. How do you feel about your own approach to death? (Chapter 11)

10. Who or what is Jesus for you? (Chapter 11)

Final Word

Two quotations summarise this book.

First is from a marvellous wordsmith, story-teller, theologian. He tells of the one who is to become Alfred the Great, but at this stage of the story is a poor Christian visitor to the chiefs of the invading Norsemen, with their love of arson and bad theology. He has no political, military, or financial power or status, but is defiant in the claim of the one true God, the Creator who was willing to go to death. This is the wisdom to disarm all ideologies of destruction, fascist, Nazi, apartheid, or finance-worship. (You must read it aloud, let its rhythms and resonances work.):

> Therefore your end is on you,
> Is on you and your kings;
> Not for a fire on Ely fen,
> Not that your gods are nine or ten,
> But because it is only Christian men
> Guard even heathen things.
>
> For our God has blessed creation,
> Calling it good. I know
> What spirit with whom you blindly band
> Hath blessed destruction with his hand;

Yet by God's death the stars still stand,
And the small apples grow.

(G. K. Chesterton, *The Ballad of the White Horse,* in *Poems for All Purposes* (London, Pimlico 1994), 106.

And second, the strongest truth, from one who has been for me, for 55 years, friend, colleague, and inspiration:

Goodness is stronger than evil.
Love is stronger than hate;
Light is stronger than darkness,
Life is stronger than death.
Victory is ours,
Though him who loved us.

(Desmond Tutu, arranged by John L. Bell with music, in *There is One Among Us* (Glasgow, Iona Community, Wild Goose Worship Group 1995), 30.

Author

John Dudley Davies: born 1927, Merseyside. RAF 1945–48. Cambridge University (BA 1951, MA 1963). Theological College at Lincoln. Ordained deacon 1953; priest 1954 (curate at Halton, Leeds). Married Shirley 1956. South Africa 1956–1970 (mission priest in Eastern Transvaal and Zululand, 1956–63; university chaplain and member of ecumenical agencies 1963–70; residence and ministry permission withdrawn by South African government, 1970). Staff of Church of England Board of Education 1970–1974. Vicar and chaplain, Keele 1974–76. Principal of College of Ascension, Birmingham, 1976–81. Cathedral Canon and Mid-Wales parish priest, Diocese of St Asaph 1981–86. Anglican Bishop of Shrewsbury 1987. Retired 1994, first to North Wales, then to Shropshire. Community councillor and parish councillor between 1984 and 2016. Honorary Assistant Bishop of St Asaph from 2009. Author of more than ten published books, mainly about practical interpretation of the Bible. We have three children (all born in South Africa), five grandchildren and three great-grandchildren. I use my full name in Wales, because there are three of us in Wales who are designated Bishop John Davies, and the other two are much more distinguished than I.